Haunted Nevada City
and
Grass Valley

Front cover image created by Tim Myers

Haunted Nevada City
and
Grass Valley

Mark Lyon

Windwhistle Press

First Edition

ISBN 978-0-9795327-7-1

To those who so kindly shared their ghostly encounters with me and to those who, over the years, have supported my Haunted Nevada City and Haunted Grass Valley tours, this book is most gratefully dedicated.

Also available from Windwhistle Press

The Young Ghost Hunter's Handbook
By Mark Lyon

San Francisco Ghosts
By Mark Lyon

The Grey Ghost Book
By Jessie Adelaide Middleton

Another Grey Ghost Book
By Jessie Adelaide Middleton

The White Ghost Book
By Jessie Adelaide Middleton

Leap Castle
The House of Horrors
The Most Haunted Castle in Ireland
By Mildred Darby
With an Introduction by Mark Lyon

Preface

As darkness falls and shadows lengthen, Nevada City, illuminated by flickering gas streetlights, and Grass Valley, with its more rough and tumble Gold Rush era ambience, become the perfect settings for a ghost story. Or, perhaps, I should say ghost stories for these towns harbor far more than their fair share of lingering spirits and numerous homes and storefronts conceal dark secrets behind their carefully restored and attractively painted exteriors.

In fact, if a proper statistical analysis could be done, I would not be at all surprised to find that, if judged by the average number of ghosts per block, Nevada City and Grass Valley might well be the most haunted towns in all of California, if not the entire American West. Why are they so haunted? Who can say? Perhaps it has something to do with their long, turbulent and sometimes violent histories. But, then, as almost everyone, tourists and locals alike, seems to love Nevada City and Grass

Valley, perhaps it is merely that some spirits simply refuse to leave.

It was at the suggestion of a friend that I first set out in search of our local ghost stories. "Someone should give a Nevada City ghost tour," she suggested following a conversation in which I had mentioned having enjoyed a fascinating historical ghost walk in Victoria, British Columbia.

The idea appealed to me as I had, for years, been relating true accounts of haunting on scores of television and radio programs and, while a graduate student, I had taught a university course on parapsychological topics.

But were there, I wondered, actually enough Nevada City hauntings to warrant a public tour? I had read a newspaper account of ghostly activity having occurred at the Nevada County Historical Society's museum in Firehouse #1 and I had heard rumors of the Red Castle Inn being haunted but that was all, hardly enough to justify an entire tour.

Delving into a folder of newspaper and magazine clippings at the Doris Foley Library for Historical Research, I unearthed a few promising accounts and, thus encouraged, I began to ask Nevada City store and restaurant proprietors, "Has anything strange, anything which you cannot account for in the way of a 'natural' explanation, ever occurred in your building?"

I was amazed by how often the person to whom I posed my query would answer, "How did you know?" or would reply, "Not in my building but ask next door. They'll tell you a story you won't believe!" And soon I had compiled more than enough accounts of haunted sites in Nevada City to create a proper tour.

My initial plan had been to offer a limited number of Saturday night tours in July and August of 2004. Little could I have guessed that the tour dates would be extended through Halloween nor could I have possibly imagined that I would continue to offer tours for at least another eighteen years or that, two years later, I would be asked to add a Haunted Grass Valley tour. Even more surprising was the fact that people began to come to me sharing so many of their own first-hand accounts of local haunting that, one day, there would be enough stories to justify an entire book!

Now, you may be asking yourself, are all of the stories I am about to share with you true? I can't really claim to know. What I can tell you, however, is that every story which I shall relate has either been given the dubious imprimatur of previously being recorded in print or it was told to me personally by someone who either encountered the ghost themselves or who had heard the story from someone else who vouched for its veracity.

Might you actually encounter a ghost or two in Nevada City or Grass Valley? Well, that's equally hard to say. Ghosts are notoriously fickle entities, appearing to one person while remaining undetectable to another, sometimes remaining inactive for decades only to unexpectedly reappear when renovations are made to the building in which they reside. Furthermore, the fact of a site once being haunted does not necessarily mean that it is still haunted today. While some ghosts seem to stay forever, others tend to fade away with time. With that being said, let us begin.

Mark Lyon
Nevada City
2021

Contents

Haunted Grass Valley

Haunted Nevada City

Nevada City's Beginnings

Nevada City's origins began on the banks of Deer Creek in the fall of 1849 with the arrival of the first gold miners. At that time the settlement was known as Deer Creek Dry Diggins and miners were said to have extracted as much as a pound of gold per day from this one creek.

In March of 1850 a meeting was called to rename the town whose population had, by then, swelled to over ten thousand. The name Nevada (Spanish for "snowy") was chosen in remembrance of the unusually hard winter they had just recently survived. In 1864, however, the townspeople had to meet again to rename their town. A former fellow resident, William Morris Stewart, who was to later become the first United States senator from the state of Nevada, had liked the name and, upon moving to the territory which was to, one day, become the state of Nevada, he thoughtlessly bestowed our town's name upon the newly incorporated territory. In order to avoid confusion on the part of the postal authorities, the townspeople reluctantly added the word "City" to the town's name.

The Pine Grove Cemetery

It is, perhaps, fitting that we start with one of Nevada City's oldest cemeteries, the Pine Grove Cemetery, established in 1851 on Red Dog Road, where many of the town's early citizens were interred; including among them, Lyman Gilmore, who claimed to have achieved flight in a steam-powered airplane of his own design on May 15, 1902, nineteen months before the Wright Brothers' first powered flight.

A young woman whom I met while collecting local ghost stories told me of driving out to the cemetery one night with her boyfriend. They parked on Red Dog just beyond the cemetery's eastern boundary with the intention of, shall we say, enjoying each other's company. But no sooner had they parked than they heard the eerie sound of a bell tolling from deep within the cemetery. The sound so unnerved the couple that they immediately changed their plans and drove away as quickly as possible.

Many years ago, another woman showed me an intriguing photograph which she had taken while visiting the old cemetery. A large mass of swirling, white cloud-like vapors filled the top portion of the photograph and what appeared to possibly be faces could be seen floating in the background. The photograph did not seem to be a double exposure and I could not discover any "natural" explanation for what appeared to be paranormal phenomena.

The Lone Pine Grave

Another haunted cemetery once existed in an area of Nevada City known as Cement Hill. In 1888 the residents of Cement Hill, said to be of sound and sober minds, reported seeing the ghosts of a young woman and her infant daughter walking hand in hand amongst the evergreens which framed their lonely grave on a slope of the hill. Shining lights were said to filter down from the heavens and hover above the grave while the voice of the mother could be heard interacting with the babbling of her child and segments of an exquisitely beautiful melody, perhaps a lullaby, were said to waft on the evening breeze.

Those who had known her in life stated that the woman had come to Cement Hill in the 1850's with her young prospector husband. The beautiful young woman, who had been adored by the other miners, succumbed to the hand of death at a tragically early age. While on her deathbed, her husband had promised he would, one day, take her body back East so that she might be interred next to the grave of her mother. The promise was made but it was never to be fulfilled. She was buried on Cement Hill with her stillborn baby placed gently upon her breast.

Throughout the 1880's, every spring an array of the earliest and most fragrant wildflower blossoms was found to have been scattered over her grave by the hand of an unknown admirer, a burial site which would, forever, be known as "The Lone Pine Grave."

The Martin Luther Marsh House

Among those interred in the Pine Grove Cemetery are the mortal remains of Martin Luther Marsh. And, if you were to walk from the cemetery towards town, you would see, at 254 Boulder Street, set back within beautifully tended grounds and marked with an historical marker, one of Nevada City's most elegantly designed historical homes, the Martin Luther Marsh House. Built in 1873 by the lumber baron for his wife, Emma Ann Ward Marsh, the house was conveniently situated directly across the street from his lumber mill.

A week or so before the Marsh family was to move in, tragedy struck. On July 8, 1873 Emma died from a miscarriage and peritonitis following a fall from a ladder sustained while she was measuring the front library windows for draperies. It is thought that, in death, she haunts the house she was never able to enjoy in life.

A previous owner of the house, Carol Fluke, once recalled a time when her mother, Ruthe Hamm, was living in the house and gave historical tours of the house to the public. One day, after the last visitors had departed and Ruthe was enjoying her afternoon tea, she heard footsteps upstairs in the hallway. Thinking an errant visitor had remained upstairs, she climbed the staircase in search of the lingering guest. Upon doing so, however, she found no one there. Although this occurred almost every day over a prolonged period of time, the bewildered older lady chose not to mention it to her daughter or to anyone else for fear that they would think she was, as her daughter put it, "getting dotty."

But, then, Carol and her husband, David, while visiting the house with a friend, were to have their own dramatic encounter with the unexplained. Just as they were about to retire to bed after a late night dinner, they a heard a bedroom door open followed by footsteps in the hallway, seemingly moving from one room to another. 'Oh, gosh," Carol said to her husband, "our friend must be ill." But, upon checking in on the friend, Carol found their guest to be in bed and wide awake. She had heard the footsteps as well and she had thought that it had been Carol or David. Upon Carol telling her that neither she nor her husband had been out of their room, they did the only thing appropriate in such a situation. Both ladies screamed in terror.

When, the next morning, they related their experience to Carol's mother, she was not in the least surprised, calmly explaining that this happened every night. She had even seen the spirits and she felt quite certain that they were friendly. Ruthe explained that the ghosts were a mother and her children, the mother moving from bedroom to bedroom, opening doors and pointing, as if telling each child in turn, "This will be your room."

Could this, perhaps, be the spirit of Emma Marsh imagining the life she had hoped to share with her four children in the house? Or, perhaps, the ghostly lady could be Mrs. Bishop, the housekeeper who raised the Marsh children following their mother's death. For years, whenever Carol and her husband visited the house, they heard the footsteps. Once they moved into the house with their own children, however, the sound of the phantom footsteps ceased.

And then there is the ghost of the man with the whiskey bottle. One morning a houseguest of the Flukes who had taken to sleeping in the back yard during a heat wave complained that she just could not put up with what she called their "friend" one night longer.

"What do you mean, our 'friend'?" Carol asked.

Each morning, at around three-thirty, she had awakened to the sound of dogs howling and she had observed a man whom she had assumed to be a friend of her hosts taking a shortcut through the yard. The man would draw near to where the houseguest slept, stare her a moment, a leering grin upon his lips, pull the cork from a whisky bottle he carried, take a swig from the bottle and, then, continue on his way through the yard and across the street.

"That was no friend of ours!" Carol responded and, when they investigated later that morning, they found that it would have been impossible for anyone to have taken the path their houseguest had described as a substantial fence would have prohibited an intruder from entering the yard at the point from which the leering man had been observed to have emerged.

And then there was the man's whiskey bottle. As Carol pointed out, who in this day and age would carry a whisky bottle with a cork stopper in it?

For a time the Marsh House served as a bed and breakfast inn; an inn offering a personal service which most guests might prefer to do without — a ghost which, on occasion, would crawl into a guest's bed!

140 Boulder Street

In 1895 the recent graduate of Stanford University and future thirty-first president of the United States, Herbert Hoover, rented a room for a period of time in the house at 140 Boulder Street while he attempted to gain practical experience in mining by working at both the Mayflower and the Reward mines for approximately two dollars a day.

One of the bedrooms in this house is said to be haunted by the ghost of a young boy with his hair in a pigtail and wearing a white ruffled shirt. The ghost reportedly appears in the early morning hours standing in front of the bed shaking his head in what I can only assume to be a rather disconcerting manner.

The Nevada Brewery Building

At 107 Sacramento Street stands what was once the Nevada Brewery, constructed in 1882 from locally quarried granite upon the site of an earlier brewery dating to 1857. Following the brewery's closure in 1899, the building served at various times over the decades as a stable, a dance hall, a bowling alley, a law office and, most recently, as a restaurant.

With such a long and varied history, it should come as no surprise that the building might be haunted. A former bartender who had worked in the building told me of personal encounters with an extremely foul smelling phantom which often manifested itself in a room behind the bar on the first floor late at night as he was closing up. It was described as a pungent, "funky" smell similar to that of rotting garbage. Even upon those much appreciated nights when the horrific smell failed to materialize, the bartender spoke of often feeling unexplainably uncomfortable late at night while working alone in the building.

The bartender also spoke of another ghost which has been observed sitting at the bar. He appears in the form of a man dressed as a miner. This phantom seems so substantial to those who have seen it as to be mistaken for a flesh and blood patron until one observes him more closely and sees that his legs disappear from his knees on down.

A former cook told me of seeing a heavy culinary grinder inexplicably rise up into the air and fly across the kitchen, hurling itself into a wall.

The manager of a previous restaurant in the building told me of, early in the morning, hearing doors open and close on the second floor although no one was upstairs at the time. And a former owner of the building who, at the time, slept on the third floor, told me of seeing a woman in Victorian clothing standing at the foot of her bed in the middle of the night.

If you visit the courtyard at the back of the building, you will see what remains of a large tunnel which was used to condition barrels of ale; a tunnel which, at one time, is believed by many to have connected to a tunnel leading to Nevada City's commercial district. Although there is some controversy regarding what I am about to disclose, it is said that, at a time in the very distant past when the brewery building served as a restaurant, men dining there with their unsuspecting wives would sometimes excuse themselves, duck into the tunnel and make their way under Deer Creek to the tunnel's opening onto Spring Street behind the National Hotel, where they enjoyed a brief interlude with the "soiled doves" who plied their trade in the many brothels which, then, lined Spring Street. How the men would have explained so long an absence from the table was not recorded.

It is also possible that the tunnels associated with the brewery were used for far darker purposes. In an era when the Chinese were often treated with extreme cruelty in California's gold mining towns, it has been alleged by some that a group of Chinese men were confined in an offshoot of the main brewery tunnel which was then dynamited, burying the men alive. Some claim this was due to a tunnel cave in trapping the workers inside and the tunnel owner not wanting to expend the time and money which would have been required to try to rescue them. Others claim this was done in order to avoid paying the workers their back wages. This may explain why there have been reports of Chinese ghosts haunting the vicinity of the brewery building.

While the reason for which the many tunnels which, to this day, lie beneath much of downtown Nevada City were built is a matter of dispute, a former owner of the brewery building told me that, many years ago, she met an elderly gentleman who told her that, when he was a boy, he once descended down into a tunnel opening near the brewery building and he was able to walk via the tunnel under Deer Creek and continue on until it ended in a basement somewhere in the Chinese Quarter on Commercial Street.

The Plaza Grocery Building

Directly across the street from the Nevada Brewery Building, at 101 Broad Street, is the Plaza Grocery Building, a building which, in its time, has gone through numerous incarnations. Previous to its construction, this area had been the site of the Jenny Lind Theatre which, supported by timber pilings, jutted out over Deer Creek. Opening on November 20, 1851, the Jenny Lind was to last only a few months. On March 3, 1852, an unusually fierce storm transformed the normally placid Deer Creek into a raging torrent overflowing its banks and sweeping away everything in its path. A log smashed into one of the Jenny Lind's pilings and, not long thereafter, amidst shouts of "There she goes!" the theater broke loose from its supports and floated away down the creek.

From 1882 through 1973, the present building served as the Plaza Grocery, an establishment which boasted of having a water powered elevator, not surprisingly, the only water powered elevator in Nevada County.

In the 1970's and on into the 1980's the Plaza Grocery building housed a restaurant called The Jacks, so named because it's two owners were both named Jack. There was Jack Beggs, known as "Little Jack," and Jack Wentz, known as "Big Jack." Chandeliers hanging in one particular dining room would often flash on and off quickly, "almost like a strobe light," Jack Beggs once recalled. The ghost must have liked an audience, however, as the phantom lightshow would occur only when there were, according to Little Jack, "a lot of people" in the room.

And then there was the figure which Beggs felt to be a lady which appeared on numerous occasions in a thirteen foot high, gold framed pier mirror which, in those days, graced one of the dining rooms. Both Beggs and a number of his customers saw the phantom. So many of their customers saw the figure in the mirror that a number of them flatly refused to ever dine in that room again. While the specter's face was "not clear," they distinctly observed it to be wearing what Beggs described as a grey "hooded, cape-like thing."

But, then, it might have been the mirror which was haunted rather than that particular dining room as this was a mirror with a curious origin story. One day a woman entered an antiques shop on Broad Street owned by the local historian and collector of early California artifacts, Don Schmitz.

"I want you to sell that mirror for me," the woman flatly stated in a manner which brooked no dissention while pointing to an extremely tall mirror on the bed of a truck parked just outside the shop. Schmitz told me that he was far from eager to accept the mirror as he knew its size would make it extremely difficult to sell. But, before he had a chance to express his misgivings, Little Jack, who, at that very moment, had been walking up the street, entered the shop.

"How much do you want for the pier mirror on the truck?" he asked.

A deal was quickly struck and the truck was backed down Broad Street to The Jacks where it was soon installed in the dining room. Could it have been that the previous owner, so insistent on ridding herself of the mirror, had also seen a ghostly figure in the mirror?

Whether it was the mirror which was haunted or the dining room, itself, there is no question that the Plaza Grocery building is haunted. Once, after the restaurant had been locked up and the burglar alarm set for the night, Little Jack and a few members of his staff were enjoying a nightcap in the downstairs bar when they heard the sound of footsteps, someone walking back and forth in the restaurant just above them. They next heard the loud sound of dishes clattering together. Thinking someone had secreted himself in the restaurant in the hope of robbing the place, Little Jack called the police who searched the restaurant thoroughly. No intruder was found although Beggs maintained that "no one could have gotten out without activating the burglar alarm."

When, years later, the restaurant changed hands, becoming the Creekside Café, the ghostly phenomena continued unabated. Doors would continually open and close of their own accord in a downstairs area which then served as a cabaret and it was in this portion of the building that Bill Sullivan, one of the new owners, saw a ghost he nicknamed, "Fred," a scruffy looking man dressed in a work shirt and work pants whom Bill thought might be a miner. When he and his partner, Richard Farrar, renovated the building, putting in a kitchen and a fireplace downstairs, Bill felt that Fred should have a room of his own where he would not be disturbed by either the customers or his staff. So Bill created and sealed off an empty space behind the new fireplace and dubbed it "Fred's room." This must have been all that the ghost wanted for Fred was not reported as being seen again until, years later, when the building again changed hands and served as a Mexican restaurant called Los Amigos. A member of the staff at that time told me of often seeing Fred standing by the fireplace as well as appearing in the vicinity of the kitchen.

The Red Castle

Perched high above downtown Nevada City atop Prospect Hill is the four story red brick gothic revival fantasy known as the Red Castle, a unique home and one-time bed and breakfast inn which plays host to several ghosts.

The Red Castle was built in 1860 by John Williams for his wife Abigail. Williams and his son, Loring Wallace Williams, had struck it rich in the gold fields of Nevada City and, once completed, John, Abigail and Loring Wallace moved into the approximately four thousand square foot mansion along with Loring Wallace's new bride, Caroline Elizabeth, who, over the years, was to present him with four sons. John and Abigail were to add to the size of the family by adopting at least two, and some say more, orphans.

The Williams' loved to entertain and the house quickly became a favored gathering place of Nevada City's elite. John was elected Justice of the Peace and called "Squire Williams" by the locals while Loring Wallace would become a prominent local lawyer.

With six young children in the house, the family, it is said, decided they needed a governess and, as the story goes, one was found in the person of a small, somewhat dowdy woman whose name has sadly been lost to us through the passage of time. It is said that she loved her charges dearly and that the Williams family loved her in return and gave her a small bedroom on the fourth floor which she shared with an equally diminutive pet terrier

As time went on, one by one, members of the Williams family passed away. First John, then Loring Wallace, followed by his wife Caroline and, finally, the little governess as well. In 1891 Abigail, too tired and feeble to maintain such a large house on her own, reluctantly sold her beloved home and she is believed to have moved to Southern California to live with one of her adopted children.

By 1963 the castle had fallen upon hard times and it was purchased by Jim Schaar who set about to restore the property to its former grandeur and, upon doing so, opened the Red Castle to the public as an inn. In the course of the restoration project, both Schaar and the handyman he had hired to aid him in the task found it impossible to shake the feeling that someone was constantly watching them. Whenever they looked, however, there was no one to be seen. That was until, one day, the handyman was startled to see an elderly man materialize before him, a grave look of concern writ large across the gentleman's face. The handyman was able to observe the phantom in great detail, later describing him as "an old man ghost, in the attire of the 1880's ... a black frock coat like a judge would wear ... an old man doing a routine inspection, seeing how the work was coming along." Could it, perhaps, have been "Squire John," keeping his eye on things?

In 1963 Schaar threw a Victorian era themed New Year's Eve party at which the guests were encouraged to come in "fancy dress" to commemorate a similar party which had been given by the Williams family on Christmas in 1860. While the affair lasted well into the early morning hours, a guest by the name of Alice Erskine decided to leave the festivities early, preferring instead to sit up for a while in her room, the Gold Room, reading in bed. While doing so, she heard a knock on the door. The door opened and a lady wearing a soft grey colored Victorian dress and carrying a small terrier in her arms entered the room. Thinking the visitor was one of the guests, Alice conversed amiably with the woman about the party and other subjects of mutual interest while the lady in grey sat at the foot of the bed petting her dog. After a while the visitor got up, said "Everything is going to be fine!" turned round and left the room, closing the door behind her.

The next morning Alice was surprised to find that her late night visitor was not to be found among those assembled for breakfast. Upon relating her story, Alice was stunned to learn that everyone who had attended the party was currently present in the dining room and that no dog had been seen at any time during the course of the evening!

Ever since the "Lady in Grey" has been seen quite often in the Gold Room as well as in other bedrooms, the hallways, and, most frequently of all, on the fourth floor where she and the children had slept. Guests staying on the fourth floor often told of feeling phantom hands gently stroke their hair, of awakening in the middle of the night to see someone standing at the foot of their bed or of seeing unexplainable discs of light flit about their room.

From 1978 to 1985 Chris Dickman and Jerry Ames had ownership of the Red Castle, also running it as a bed and breakfast inn. Although neither of them ever saw an apparition, they were not exempt from experiencing unexplainable phenomena. As Chris put it, the Red Castle "hid things." He would put things away in their appropriate places only to find, when he later went back to retrieve the items, that they were not where he was quite certain he had left them. Sometimes he would subsequently discover the missing objects in an entirely different part of the house.

One day, following a snow storm, a guest asked, "Who is that man on the deck? He's dressed rather strangely in black and wearing a tall hat." As the description did not fit any of their guests, Chris and Jerry went out to investigate. No one was on the deck and no one could have been on the deck, no flesh and blood intruder at any rate, as not one single footprint could be found upon the eighteen inch deep blanket of snow covering the deck.

And then there was the ashen faced guest who, after spending the night in the Gold Room, asked, "Who is David?"

He was asleep in his bed, the guest explained, when he was awakened by pressure on his legs. As he began to get his bearings, he realized that he couldn't move his legs because someone was sitting on them. He opened his eyes and saw a woman sitting on the corner of the bed. She was dressed in grey and seemed angry. "David! David!" she said, as if to reprimand a disobedient child. The lady swiftly faded away and the pressure on his legs lifted immediately, as if someone had gotten up off them.

On another occasion two guests returning back to their room following dinner were more than a bit shaken to see the figure of a lady pass through the closed door of the Gold Room, make her way across the hall and effortlessly glide through a closed door into the Rose Room.

That portion of hallway between the Gold Room and the Rose Room seems to be particularly haunted as a visitor was once startled to observe a number of figures, all dressed in nineteenth century clothing, passing from the Gold Room into the Rose Room and from the Rose Room into the Gold Room.

The next couple to own the house, running it for twenty-nine years as a bed and breakfast inn, was Mary Louise and Conley Weaver. They also reported having their own share of paranormal experiences. One night a couple staying in the Grey Lady's bedroom saw a strange light appear in their room although no lights were on in the house at the time. The light circled around the foot of the bed and, then, inexplicably, vanished.

Another guest reported seeing a woman dressed in Victorian attire walking in the garden at night.

The Weavers told of an employee seeing a ghost wearing a Civil War era uniform in one of the bedrooms while, on another occasion, they were mystified to find the door to the third floor balcony locked from the outside, an occurrence they were hard pressed to explain as there are no stairs, trellises or any other means by which one might have escaped from the balcony once he had locked the door.

On yet another occasion Conley heard the sound of someone playing a bugle, only later did he learn that Loring Wallace Williams was known to have had a habit of playing a bugle while standing on the fourth floor balcony.

A former employee told me that doors to the buffet in the dining room often opened by themselves as did drawers in the kitchen and that she once observed the door to the Rose Room to be slammed shut by invisible forces. She also recalled the day a speaker employed to allow the staff to hear the doorbell while working downstairs moved from where it had been placed on the kitchen stove onto the top of a stepladder.

One of the ghosts, however, could be most helpful at times. One day my informant was putting sheets in a linen closet when she found that the vacuum cleaner was in her way. She put down her stack of sheets with the intention of moving the vacuum but, as she did so, she heard the distinct sound of a large object being moved. When she looked up, she was pleased to find that the vacuum had been moved out of the way for her.

On still another occasion, while waiting downstairs for the laundry to finish its cycle, one of her coworkers suggested that they turn on the television. No sooner had the suggestion been made than the television turned on by itself.

The Aristocrat Hill Ghost

A retired law enforcement officer related to me the details of a ghostly incident which he, himself, had witnessed concerning a stately Victorian home in a residential area dating back to the town's gold rush beginnings known as "Aristocrat Hill"; a home which belonged to a family which regularly left the house during the winter, spending those months living in the San Francisco Bay Area.

It was a cold night in January or February when the burglar alarm went off in the securely locked and unoccupied house. When the police arrived they saw that French doors off a second floor bedroom were standing wide open. As the owners of the house had left a set of keys with the police, the officers were able to enter and thoroughly search the house. Once they had assured themselves that no one was in the house, the police closed and secured the French doors, locked up the house and returned to the police station.

Forty-five minutes to an hour later, the alarm went off again and, again, the police made their way back to the house. Again, the French doors were standing wide open and, once again, the police made their way to the bedroom. One of the officers then noticed a man's leather belt lying on the bed and he decided to tie the handles of the doors together with the belt. This being done, the police again locked up the house and left.

Forty-five minutes to an hour later, the alarm went off for a third time and, for a third time, the police made their way back to the house. For a third time, the French doors were standing wide open. When they entered the bedroom, the belt with which they had attempted to secure the doors was back on the bed where they had initially found it.

The National Exchange Hotel

The National Exchange Hotel at 211 Broad Street, which is actually composed of three buildings which were constructed in the years 1854, 1856 and 1857, is believed to be one of the oldest hotels in continuous operation west of the Rocky Mountains and it was frequented by such luminaries as Mark Twain, Lotta Crabtree (the highest paid actress of her era and known as "The Nation's Darling"), the notorious Lola Montez and the future thirty-first president of the United States, Herbert Hoover.

A lady named Yvonne, who worked in the National Hotel dining room in 1988, told me that, while opening the restaurant in the morning, she would often feel a cold gust of air rush by her and hear a voice whisper, "Yvonne! Yvonne!" It was a rather playful ghost. It would lift her ponytail up into the air or pull playfully on one of her earlobes.

Once, as she opened up in the morning, she heard what she thought was the restaurant's stereo sound system playing at an unusually high volume. She proceeded to turn down the volume, only to find that the stereo was not on.

A chef working at the restaurant was so unnerved upon feeling an unseen hand placed upon his shoulder while washing dishes at the end of the dinner service that he quit on the spot, fleeing the kitchen without finishing the task at hand and leaving a very expensive set of knives, the tools of his trade, behind in the restaurant. He never returned to retrieve his knives.

And then there was the gentleman who told me of how, one evening while dining at the National with his wife, a child's ball flew into the dining room, sailing under their table without coming out the other side. This was followed by a little girl dressed in Victorian clothes running into the dining room and diving under the table as if after the ball. The man turned to his wife and asked, "Did you see what I just saw?"

"Yes," she answered as they gingerly lifted up the tablecloth only to find neither the ball nor the little girl.

It is probable that it was this same little girl who was responsible for drawers and doors in the lower parts of the cabinetry which, at the time, lined one of the dining room walls being opened by unseen hands. The drawers and doors higher up in the cabinetry, however, were never observed to fly open, leading to speculation that they were too high for the little girl ghost to reach.

On one occasion a glass goblet in the dining room shattered when no one was near it and, sometimes, as the dining room lights were turned out upon closing at night, a single note would be heard to issue from the dining room's grand piano.

A former server told me of seeing a woman in Victorian attire float across the dining room. Perhaps it is the same ghostly Victorian woman who was also seen, from time to time, leaning against the green upright piano which, in those days, stood against a wall in the adjoining barroom. Those who saw her said she looked as if she was about to sing a song. Those who have seen this ghost have also reported that she resembled the woman in a large antique photographic portrait which hung for decades in the dining room, a stern looking woman wearing a high-collared Victorian blouse. A woman fitting this same description, only this time reading a book, mysteriously appeared in a photograph which was taken of the, at the time unoccupied, seating area near one of the hotel bar's front windows.

However, the Victorian lady is not the only ghost to haunt the National's bar. A former bartender told me of the night when, close to closing time, as there were no longer any customers to serve, he stood alone behind the bar watching television until it was time to lock up. He then heard the muffled voices of a man and a woman behind him. He turned around to serve them but there was no one there to be seen. The voices, however, continued. As he moved toward the area from which the voices seemed to be coming, they moved just a bit beyond him. He chased the voices throughout the room as they stubbornly continued to move away from him. In the end he was unable to find anyone or anything to account for the curious happening.

Another bartender reported how, as he left the bar by way of the dining room one night after closing, he suddenly remembered that he had forgotten a task which he needed to accomplish before leaving. As he crossed back into the dining room, he felt himself enveloped in a freezing coldness, as if he had stepped into a walk-in freezer. The intense cold surrounded him as he passed through the dining room, back into the bar and into the storage room behind the bar where he finished his task as quickly as possible. The horrific cold continued to follow him as he left the barroom, not leaving him until he had exited past the dining room.

Yet another bartender told me of how, when she opened up the bar one morning, upon beginning her set-up procedure behind the bar, she heard a distinct creaking sound coming from one of two pairs of glass doors, which prior the recent hotel's remodeling, existed between the bar and the dining room, a pair of doors which were always kept closed. One of the two doors which were always kept closed was now standing wide open. She walked across the barroom and closed the door. But, no sooner had she gotten back behind the bar, than she, again, heard the creaking sound. She looked up and saw that the glass door was, again, standing open. As she knew that the barroom was haunted, she decided stronger measures needed to be taken and she locked the door in place, securing it by means of two sliding deadbolts. No sooner had she, again, made her way back to the bar, however, than she heard the creaking sound for a third time. The ghost had thrown open the deadbolts and flung the door back open for a third time.

One day some patrons at the bar were engaged in a conversation about the hotel ghosts when a man declared that there were no such things as ghosts. Immediately, a substantial nameplate holder displaying the bartender's name rose up into the air from its position behind the bar and flew violently toward the offending customer!

On another occasion a customer felt an understandable chill as a pair of phantom arms wrapped themselves closely around her.

But the ghosts in the bar and the dining room are but a few of the National's resident ghosts. Ghostly footsteps have often been heard in the hallway on the second floor leading from the area which, previously, served as the hotel lobby.

An elderly man in Victorian clothes has been seen sitting in the former lobby while a recent guest told me of encountering a dapper Victorian era gentleman on a hotel staircase who, upon passing partially through her, stopped, turned and politely said, "Pardon me, Madam."

A little girl matching the description of the ghostly girl observed in the dining room has also been seen playfully bouncing a ball, jumping rope and riding a tricycle in the hotel hallways.

A "washed out" appearing "White Lady" in a long Victorian dress with a yellow sash, her hair styled up on her head in an old-fashioned manner, has been seen floating several inches above the floor in one of the guestrooms as well as having been observed proceeding down the third floor hallway only to pass through a closed door into a Broad Street facing room. Some who have seen her have remarked that she smells of the cheap perfume favored by the "ladies of the evening" who worked in the many brothels which, in Nevada City's early days, were conveniently located directly behind the hotel.

A part of the hotel with a particularly disturbing reputation is the area at the eastern end of the second floor hallway, a space now divided into two luxuriously appointed rooms, Room 208 and Room 209. For decades, this space was occupied by the hotel's Presidential Suite. Many years ago, a business party of eight checked into the National, each member of the group having been assigned his own room. The leader of the group took, for himself, the Presidential Suite with its fireplace, antique furnishings and separate sitting room. The group met for their afternoon meeting in the Presidential Suite and all seemed well throughout the day but, upon returning to his room after dinner, the group's chairman came rushing down to the reception desk appearing as white as — well — a ghost and he asked if he might have another room. He was informed that another room was available but, as they had already used the Presidential Suite earlier in the day, he would be charged for the second room. "That's alright," he responded. "That's alright. Just as long as I never have to go back into that room again!" He was so frightened that he refused to reenter the room briefly enough to retrieve his luggage and other personal effects, requiring the hotel staff to bring his belongings to him. He never explained what he had experienced in the Presidential Suite but he was not to be alone in this regard.

A local restaurateur once had relatives visiting from out of town. Wanting to treat them extremely well, he booked them into the Presidential Suite. They were only in the room for a few minutes before they checked out and, not long thereafter, appeared on his doorstep declaring, "We're staying with you!"

In yet another case, frightened hotel guests packed up their belonging in the middle of the night and fled their room in terror. Which room they had occupied is lost to memory but there is more than a good chance that it was the Presidential Suite.

The mystery as to why guests had so hastily fled the room may have finally been solved when, a few years ago, two ladies told me of their experience. They had been walking past the door to the Presidential Suite; a door in which, at that time, there was a large glass panel covered on the inside by a curtain. The two ladies saw a hand had pulled back the curtain and staring at them from inside the room was a woman with a pinched face wearing a high-collared Victorian blouse; a woman whose description was eerily similar to that of the woman whose antique photographic portrait, at that time, hung in the hotel dining room. Then, moments later, both ladies clearly observed the Victorian lady to slowly dissolve into nothingness!

Another room with a ghostly reputation is Room 314. It was in this room that sometime in the 1890's, three men, Eugene de Sabla, Jr., Alfonso Tregidgo, and John Martin, met to discuss the possibility of harnessing hydroelectric power from a powerhouse above Nevada City on the South Fork of the Yuba River. After joining forces with the grandson of the founder of the Colgate Soap & Perfume Company, Romulus Riggs Colgate, their plans led to the formation of what would, one day, become the Pacific Gas and Electric Company.

Years ago, a well respected business woman staying in this room awoke one night to see men attired in late nineteenth century clothing consulting maps, conversing in an enthusiastic manner and smoking cigars. Rather than being frightened, she was fascinated and watched the phantom scene until, at length, it melted away. The lady was so intrigued by the experience that, on a latter visit, she booked the same room, hoping to repeat her ghostly encounter.

Whether she was able to view the ghostly meeting a second time is unknown, but what is known is that previous members of the hotel staff saw the National's ghosts so often that the housekeepers would often make deals among themselves, saying, "I will clean the scary room you don't like if you will take care of the creepy room I don't like."

According to an unverifiable legend, a little girl called Elizabeth died from the mumps or some other disease in Room 411 in one of the cottages located at the back of the hotel. Guests staying in this room have, at times, been said to have felt her presence in the room. Other guests have claimed that an antique, watercolor tinted photograph of a little girl which, at the time, hung on a wall in Room 411 would, in the middle of the night, take on life-like living hues. Whether there is truth to any of this or not, it is true that the housekeeping staff, when they proceeded to clean the room in the morning, would often find that the photograph had been taken off the wall and turned upside-down onto a table and guests who had stayed in that room, upon checking out, would sometimes remark to the desk clerk, "You really need to get rid of the picture of the creepy little girl!" What happened to this photograph upon the sale and renovation of the hotel is currently unknown.

And then, finally, there is the mystery of the locked room. Many years ago there was a gentleman employed at the hotel as a handyman who, also at times, manned the check-in desk in the area of the second floor which previously served as the hotel's lobby. As well as being given a salary, he was given a hotel room on the third floor in which he lived. When, one day, the handyman died, Tom Coleman, the then owner of the National, locked the door to that room and the door remained locked for well over a decade until the hotel was sold in 2018.

It was during those years that a member of the hotel staff related to me how, often upon passing the locked door, he would hear the sound of footsteps inside the room and, if he was passing by at precisely the right time, he would hear the footsteps pass through the locked door, proceed down the hallway and descend the staircase; the treads creaking as the unseen entity made its way down to the lobby where it ended its journey behind the reception desk.

When, in 2018, the current owners began the restoration and remodeling of the hotel, the locked room was, at last, opened. The room was exactly as it had been at the time of the handyman's death. A carefully preserved uniform from the First World War was found hanging in the closet.

Calanan Park

Directly across the street from the National Exchange Hotel and featuring a hydraulic mining nozzle, an ore car and other artifacts from Nevada County's mining history is Calanan Park. For a number of years Miriam Morris has, on a volunteer basis, tended to the upkeep of the park, as well as adding a garden, a charming interactive children's section and other artistic elements to the park. She has also researched the park's history.

"I am convinced," she wrote to me, "that Charles Kent and George Calanan both inhabit the park on occasion. Charles Kent was one of the early inhabitants of Nevada City. He was a sheriff and then a state senator. He owned a butcher shop about where the DA's office is and used part of the property the park is on as a stable and hog processing area."

Unfortunately, during his tenure as a state senator, Kent became both an alcoholic and addicted to horserace gambling, often "disappearing" from time to time. An old newspaper article Miriam found concerning one of his disappearances optimistically opined "we are sure old Chuck will return."

Continuing with Ms. Morris' account, "He later lost all his money, his butcher shop, his house on Nevada Street, his wife died and, the following spring in 1890, he threw himself off a ferry in the San Francisco bay. His body was discovered the following day.

"Sometimes when I'm working in the park, I will detect the smell of rotting meat. I look all over and find nothing. A few times, the sprinklers will turn on at a time when they aren't supposed to. I'm not sure I like Charles Kent's spirit that much. He is too unhappy. However, I am inclined to attribute the disappearance of a few troublemakers to his intervention. Maybe he is trying to atone for his past.

"George Calanan, for whom the park is named, also owned the butcher shop, much later. George is a sunnier and lighter spirit. I feel him watching over the park trying to keep bad things from happening. One time on a Christmas morning, one of the street people stopped at the drinking fountain for a drink. The drinking fountain was turned off for the winter, but somehow, it went on for this person. I checked and the water was turned off. I think George wanted him to have a drink.

"George's wife, Lena, was one of the Native Daughters of the Golden West, the group that acquired the land to create the park. I think her spirit and George's called to me to come care for the severely neglected park. Whenever I'm in the park by myself, I never feel that I am alone."

The Kidd & Knox Building

On the northeast corner of Broad and North Pine Street stands the Kidd & Knox Building which, in its time, housed the law offices of two future United States senators, Aaron Augustus Sargent and William Morris Stewart and two California State Supreme Court chief justices, Niles Searls and Lorenzo Sawyer. Previous to its construction in 1856 following the Great Fire of 1856, this was the site of the Dramatic Hall in which Lola Montez performed her scandalous "Spider Dance" and such actors as Kate Hayes and Edwin Booth, arguably the greatest Shakespearian actor of the 1800's, entertained the citizens of Nevada City.

It is said that either three or four tunnels once terminated in the basement of this building, a basement painted dark by rumors. Some say it was an opium den but that is unlikely as there was a thriving opium den in the Chinese Quarter on Commercial Street.

Others have claimed that women were taken down into the basement never to be seen again, perhaps spirited out of town via the tunnels to mining camps where they were forced to toil in the "white slave" trade. There may, perhaps, be some truth to this as, before the entrances to the tunnels were sealed off, there were reports of a ghostly female form being observed within a tunnel entrance, looking as if she was calling out for help.

Stoutly built of brick with iron shutters, the building was considered to be fireproof and, during the fire of 1858, which destroyed most of the downtown area, three men fled to what they thought would be the safety of the building's basement. All might have been well if it were not for the gunpowder being stored down there. The ghastly explosion which took all three of their lives might account for some of the ghostly activity which has so often been encountered in that basement.

A young man working there many years ago was "pushed" down the basement steps by unseen forces. Another employee was terrified when a large box lifted off a shelf and flew across the basement almost striking her in the head. The manager of an earlier candy shop which did business on the premises told me of hearing her name called out by a male voice issuing from somewhere in the basement; while a more recent employee recounted an experience she would never forget. At that time, a fellow employee brought her dog to work with her, the dog happily sleeping away the day down in the basement. One day, when she had occasion to attend to a task in the basement, the dog became unaccountable agitated. The lights flickered and the young lady clearly saw a man, attired as she would imagine a miner of the 1800's to be dressed, rush past her.

But it is upstairs in the store itself that the most intriguing phenomena occur. A former manager told me of phantom footsteps being heard crossing the floor and of several times seeing a lady with long blonde hair and wearing a long, flowered dress standing where the ice cream counter is presently, her face turned away from view. On one occasion, however, the ghost turned toward the manager. Where her face should be there was only an indistinct blob! Years later an elderly lady told me that, when she was a young girl, the building housed an ice cream parlor on the first floor and the woman who owned the ice cream parlor had long blonde hair and tended to wear long, flower-patterned dresses.

A former owner of the candy shop told me that items would often move of their own accord throughout the shop. Often, upon opening up in the morning, they would find that a large number of the factory produced candy bars had been turned upside down requiring her staff to spend their morning setting everything aright again. One morning they found that a tray of handmade chocolates in a locked case had been thrown up into the air, scattering the chocolates randomly about the display case shelf.

In those days the shop sold large, clear plastic bags tied at the top with a ribbon within which were several smaller clear plastic bags, each containing a different kind of candy, each bag also being tied closed with a ribbon. One morning, upon opening up, they were shocked to discover that, although the large outer bag was still securely closed with its ribbon intact, one of the smaller inside bags, which had contained an assortment of gummy bears, was now open and the gummy bears had been dispersed throughout the larger bag.

More recently, as an employee was preparing to mop the floor prior to closing, when she reached for the mop, the trolley on which the mop and bucket of water were located violently flew approximately ten feet away from her, crashing with a bang into a door!

The Flagg Building

Directly across from the Kidd and Knox Building, at 233 Broad Street, is the Flagg Building. Built in 1856 immediately following the Great Fire of 1856 which destroyed the three-story US Hotel which had been built upon this site only three years before, the Flagg Building housed a saloon on the first floor and a hotel on the second floor. The saloon, Schreiber's Felix, was particularly known for what was referred to as "the marvelous, mysterious music box" which, it is said, entertained generations of both customers and, due to its "thunderous" volume, passersby as well with Straus waltzes and a selection from the opera *Carmen*.

In 1955 the building was sold to Eddie Furano who established a bar called Eddie's. The name was later changed to the Bank Club and, then, changed again to Eddie's Bank Club. A lady, who, at one time, had worked at the Bank Club, told me that sometimes, when opening in the morning, they would discover that phantom hands had both turned on and lit the gas burners on the grill.

Beginning in 2002, there was, for several years, a bed and breakfast inn on the second floor which, recalling the site's past, was called the US Hotel.

It was not long before the innkeepers became convinced that their establishment was haunted. A whiff of cigar smoke would sometimes float through one of the rooms while the stale odor of spent cigarettes was, on occasion, noticed in another room although the inn had long been a smoke-free establishment. Unexplainable clinking sounds, laughter and music were heard and a cool gust of wind was, at times, felt in the hallway which the owners attributed to the ghost of a young girl they called "Sarah Jane"; a ghost who they believed enjoys running up and down the hallway. Former guests were, sometimes, surprised to discover unexplainable ghostly silhouettes in photographs they had taken at the hotel.

A guest who had stayed in a room facing Broad Street told me of the afternoon when, while in his room, he heard a knock on his door. He opened the door only to find no one there although, from his vantage point, he would have easily been able to see any prankster who might have tried to knock and quickly run away. A few hours later there was, again, a knock on the door and, again, upon opening the door, there was no one to be seen.

That night, around midnight, he was awakened by the sound of footsteps just outside his door. He thought this was strange as the only other guest was staying in a room at the far end of the hotel while the innkeepers slept in a room in the attic. About an hour later, he heard the footsteps again and this was repeated for a third time an hour or so latter. When he asked at breakfast whether anyone had been walking about near his room late that night, he was told, "No." Everyone had been fast asleep in their own rooms at the time.

That guest was lucky compared to others who attempted to sleep in that room only to find the sheets, blankets and bedspread slowly pulled off them, inch by inch, until they were completely uncovered. Those guests were lucky, however, compared to the guest who, while sleeping in that room, awakened to feel cold, clammy, death-like hands gently massaging his face.

And then there was the guest who, while staying in a room at the rear of the hotel, awakened to feel someone cuddling up against his back. "How sweet of my wife," he thought. "She is just as affectionate as she was on the day we got married." Then he opened his eyes and saw that he was facing his wife. Whoever had been cuddling up against his back was not his wife! He waited awhile unable to get back to sleep. "Perhaps, I just dreamed it," he thought to himself. He was wide awake now. Then, he felt it again, someone cuddling up against his back. Only this time he realized that this was someone the size of a small child. When, at breakfast, he mentioned what he had experienced, one of the innkeepers casually remarked, "That was Sarah Jane, our little girl ghost. She likes to sleep in that bed."

Sarah Jane also liked to steal ladies' earrings, especially large hoop earrings. If a guest removed her earrings prior to going to bed and placed them on the nightstand, the earrings would often be gone in the morning. However Sarah Jane would always return them a few days later, requiring the innkeepers to keep a list of who lost what so that they could return the purloined earrings to their rightful owners by mail.

The Flume's End

Another historic building which, at one time, served as a bed and breakfast inn was the Flume's End at 317 South Pine Street. The Flume's End began life in the 1860's as a sawmill and, in later years, it was alleged to have served as a bordello.

If the later is true, perhaps one of the former *"femmes de joie"* has remained and is soliciting new clients as; one evening, a man and his wife staying at the Flume's End Inn were more than a bit nonplussed when they both heard a disembodied female voice call out the husband's name.

A guest staying in the uppermost room once complained of being awakened by a woman in what appeared to be a Victorian era wedding dress who railed bitterly and at great length to her as to how cruel life can be. It was later learned that a "lady of easy virtue" had, in Nevada City's early days, conducted her profession in that very room. Upon accepting a proposal of marriage, she had been looking forward to retiring, only to be cruelly jilted at the altar.

On another occasion, a previous owner of The Flumc's End, while unlocking the front door, was startled to observe, through one of the door's beveled glass panels, the figure of a woman in a Victorian dress glide silently across the entrance hall.

It is ghostly phenomena of very different nature, however, which makes The Flume's End unique in the annals of the paranormal. Former Nevada City Councilman and historian, Steve Contrell, disclosed to me that when he lived there many years ago, his wife often spoke of hearing the sounds of bells and violins in the house.

One evening, at a dinner party, she had the good fortune to meet a woman who had lived in the same house ten years before. "Did you ever experience anything strange when you lived there?" she asked the earlier occupant.

"You mean the bells and the violins?" The lady answered. "I heard them all the time"

The, then, owner of the Inn told me that the bells and violins were heard throughout his time in the house as well.

Could the "bells and violins" be psychic echoes from the past which, somehow, became embedded into the building from the days when it served as a sawmill? Could a saw blade cutting through lumber, perhaps, sound something like a violin and could the bells have been safety devices signaling the starting and the stopping of the saw blade?

309 Broad Street

When, years ago, this building housed Cirino's Italian restaurant, a ghostly man sitting at a table in the back of the restaurant could sometimes be seen slurping soup.

Constructed in 1890 as a saloon and featuring a bar manufactured in 1904 by the famed Brunswick-Balke-Collender Company of Chicago, the building has returned to its historic roots as the Golden Era Lounge. Cindy and Steve Giardina, the owners of the Golden Era confirmed to me that the building is, indeed, haunted. The locked rear door will sometime open by itself and, late at night, a ghostly voice can sometimes be heard emanating from the attic.

318 Broad Street

When the building at 318 Broad Street housed the popular Posh Nosh restaurant, its first owner, Fred Slikker, told me that the building was haunted by an elderly man described as wearing old-fashioned clothing and a hat whom he identified from an antique photograph as being William Henry Smith. In the 1870's, Smith occupied the building selling groceries, provisions, grain and feed. Fred so often saw the ghost casually walking from the back of the building to the area near the front door that he, one day, nailed a chair high on the wall of his office so that, as Fred put it, "the ghost would always have a place to sit."

As well as seeing the specter of the former storekeeper, staff and patrons of the restaurant often reported being tickled on the back of the neck or having their shirt collar tugged by unseen hands. And objects had an unsettling habit of falling off the walls.

While all of this has occurred on the street level portion of the restaurant, it was down in the basement where things often got more than a bit menacing. It was down there, one morning, that Fred felt a strong presence manifest itself within an inch or two of his face; a presence which, although no words were actually heard, seemed to be shouting "Get out!" And it was also in the basement that, one morning, Fred's daughter, Julie, felt an unseen entity strike her on the shoulder while, on yet another occasion, she felt a hand grasp the top of her head, frightening her so badly that she dropped an entire platter full of food. And a dark, shadow-like form has sometimes been seen flitting up the basement staircase.

When, after many years, the Posh Nosh closed its doors, building's owner, Don Schmitz, installed an antiques store in the space and, while Don adamantly denied that that the building was in any way haunted; a woman who worked for him there was equally adamant that that it was. The door to the restroom on the main floor would often open by itself. When customers who were unaware of the building's haunted reputation and had happily browsed amongst the antiques displayed on the first floor ventured down into the basement, they would often quickly return upstairs stating emphatically that the basement was haunted. At one time Don's assistant placed a recently restored and nicely varnished chair for sale in the basement. Although the chair was so delicate and fragile that it was extremely unlikely a customer would have sat in it for fear of breaking it, within a few weeks of it being in the basement, all of the varnish had been rubbed away in the places where someone sitting in it would have rested his arms.

The sense of foreboding so often felt by those who spent time in the basement may have something to do with an incident which occurred during one of Nevada City's many horrific fires. As the building's proprietor was convinced that he had a fireproof building, he decided to wait out the fire by fleeing to a space in the basement behind the pair of heavy iron doors which you may still see down there today. Although the brick walls and iron shutters did, indeed, keep the building from burning down around him, the conditions became such that either he died from asphyxiation or he was baked to death.

A few years ago a woman told me of being down in that basement when she began to feel unpleasantly warm. She next heard footsteps which began near the iron doors at the rear of the building and rushed towards her as she heard a male voice urgently shout, "Get Out!"

Could her experience explain Fred Slikker's experience so many years before? Could it be that this is not a case of a menacing ghost but, instead, that of a ghost reliving his ghastly death over and over again and trying to warn others to "get out" of the building before they might suffer his fate as well?

The New York Hotel

Although it could merely be the creaking and groaning which is to be expected from any old building, some who have worked within the historic New York Hotel, now devoted to various shops, will speak of phenomena which can be a bit unnerving. Weird noises have often been heard, the unexplainable rattling of a window and floor boards creaking beneath the carpeting as if some unseen entity were treading upon the original hardwood flooring.

Early in the morning one shop owner sometimes saw something out of the corner of her eye which would instantly vanish. And then there was the unshakable feeling of someone standing in the, otherwise, unoccupied hallway.

One evening, while conducting one of my Haunted Nevada City tours, a loud bang unexpectedly rang out like a gunshot from one of the front windows and every light in the building turned on. In the course of other tours, other unexplainable phenomena have occurred. A lady standing in front of that same window screamed when what she believed to be a ghostly hand grabbed her by the shoulder. On another evening, an item hanging on a mannequin in the display space behind that same window fell to the floor as I was speaking. On, yet, another occasion, a large wooden sign hanging above and in front of the building's entrance began to slowly swing back and forth on a breezeless night as if unseen hands were swinging it. On, still, another night, as I told my guests the story of the swinging sign, a light above the building's entrance and the two lights pointing directly toward the sign inexplicably turned on, illuminating the sign.

And, then, there was the night I heard a scream as a terrified young boy who had been sitting on a step approximately ten feet behind me was lifted into the air and thrown across the pavement, landing at my feet!

At one time there had been residential apartments up on the building's second floor. A woman who, as a child, had lived in one of those apartments told me that her mother had, at that time, a music box in her bedroom which, upon being wound and the catch released, would play as its top slowly spun round. The music box would often begin to spin and play when no one was in the room.

Strangest of all, however, was the surprise experienced by a gentleman who, at the time, owned the New York Hotel when he decided to remodel the second floor apartments into commercial office spaces. Although all of his former tenants were now gone, when he, one day, visited the building to see how the upstairs remodeling was progressing, one of workers asked, "How did she get up here?" An elderly woman was clearly seen by both men contentedly rocking back and forth in a rocking chair on the second floor balcony — a rocking chair which had not been seen in the building before.

The Nevada Theatre

In 1863 a catastrophic fire raced through Nevada City destroying the Bailey House Hotel at 401 Broad Street. Desirous of the cultural blessings a theater might provide, the Nevada Theatre Association was organized with the goal of purchasing the property and building a theater which, they hoped, would not burn to the ground. Stock in the future theater was sold at the, then, astounding price of one hundred dollars a share and, in June of 1864, a ball was held to raise additional funds. With such enthusiastic community support and bricks rescued from the remains of the Bailey House, the Nevada Theatre soon rose from the ashes, opening in the fall of 1865 with a comedy entitled *The Dutch Governor*.

Over the years such celebrities as Mark Twain, Lotta Crabtree and the opera star, Emma Nevada, (who took her stage name from Nevada City, her childhood home) have graced its stage and it remains, today, the oldest structure in California built specifically as a theater.

In 1909 the building was converted into a motion picture theater and it remained in use as such until 1959 when it was closed due to a period of economic decline and competition from television.

One hundred years after the 1863 fire which had brought the theater into being the community, again, rallied to support the cause of live theatre and a local commission was formed to raise the funds necessary to purchase and renovate the theater which has, ever since, provided a home to locally produced theatre, touring performers, lectures and a Sunday night film series.

It seems only fitting that a building with such an illustrious pedigree should offer the possibility of seeing the occasional ghost along with the live entertainment and, in this regard, the Nevada Theatre has risen to the challenge with not just one but several ghosts.

You might want to think twice before sitting in one of the invitingly cozy chairs positioned upon landings on the staircases leading up to the balcony as a ghostly woman has sometimes been seen sitting in one of those chairs.

A couple elegantly dressed in Victorian attire has been observed from time to time sitting amongst contemporary audiences and the Victorian lady was once observed backstage "borrowing" a prop during the course of a theatrical performance.

A man dressed as a cowboy of the 1800's appeared so substantial to a recent witness that he was thought to be merely someone dressed in a costume until the cowboy was seen to casually walk into and pass through a row of theater seats.

Voices can sometimes be heard coming from the stage when no one else is in the building; while down in the dressing rooms beneath the stage, you can, at times, hear footsteps on the stage above you although you know you are alone in the theater. And the door to the dressing room has been known to slam shut of its own accord.

A man working on lights in the building's attic has reported hearing a phantom voice coming from that part of the theater. Upon mentioning this to the producer of the play being mounted at the time, the producer confessed to having had exactly the same experience at a time when he had been working up there.

I have always had an unexplainable, uneasy feeling whenever I have had to spend any time up in the theater's balcony and the balcony and the area just outside the balcony doors sometimes feel inexplicably cold at times when it is warm everywhere else in the building. And, as we all know, heat rises.

The reason for my discomfort while in the balcony became clear when the business manager of a, now defunct, theatre company which often rented the theater told me of her experience one night. Part of her job entailed going down into the dressing rooms at the end of each evening performance, collecting the costumes so that she might take them to be laundered in the costume shop across the street and turning out the theater lights prior to locking the building. One night, as she was about to flick the switch which would turn out both the work lights on the stage and the lights in the house, something drew her eyes upwards where she saw a man standing near the front of the balcony. He seemed to be in his thirties. He had short dark hair and a beard and he was dressed in a black frock coat, dressed as a Victorian gentleman would have dressed for a night at the theater. The man gazed down upon her as she calmly observed him for some time. It was an extraordinary moment, one which would have sent most of us racing to the nearest exit. But the lady was not at all frightened. "I thought he had as much right to be here as I did," she later explained to me. That being the case, she calmly turned out the lights, made her way down the steps from the stage, up a now darkened theater aisle and out into the lobby, whereupon she locked the theater door and left the ghost to his own devices.

The Madison House Bed and Breakfast

The Parsonage

Ghosts who have long remained dormant sometimes suddenly make themselves known when alterations are made to their home. Such may well have been the case with the former Methodist Church parsonage at 427 Broad Street, now The Madison House Bed and Breakfast.

Built in 1865, the house was purchased in 1885 by the Nevada City Methodist Church to serve as the residence for their ministers and the ministers' families and it was utilized as such for the next eighty years. In 1986 the house was converted into a bed and breakfast inn. When subsequent innkeepers, Chuck and Susan Shea, moved in, they proceeded to make a few more changes in the physical appearance of the house, changes which seemed to stir up a spirit or two.

One day, shortly after the renovations were completed and what was then called The Parsonage reopened for business, Chuck heard a terrible commotion coming from one of the guestrooms. It sounded as if someone was hurling furniture about inside the room. The next morning Chuck apologized to the guests in the adjoining room for the noise, adding that he had no idea what the guest in the next room had been doing.

"It wasn't him" the guests informed Chuck. "We saw him leave the house before the noises started." What is more, they explained, the sounds seemed to them to be coming, not from the adjoining room, but from above them in the attic — an attic which Chuck knew to be locked and completely empty!

Chuck did not mention the incident to his wife but it would not be long before Susan was to hear the mysterious noises herself and, again, they seemed to be issuing from the attic.

Following these incidents, one morning at breakfast, a guest asked, "Who fell out of bed last night?" She had clearly heard what sounded like someone in an adjoining room falling onto the floor in the middle of the night. Upon explaining exactly where she had heard the noise, the mystery intensified as Chuck explained that there was no room on the other side of her room and that, furthermore, there was no floor upon which anyone might have fallen that night. The house had been remodeled over the years such that there is currently only an empty stairwell in that part of the house.

Perhaps the spirit or spirits of the parsonage became temporarily reconciled to their new surroundings as, for a while, all ghostly manifestations ceased. But then, after almost a year's respite, the sounds of ghostly furniture moving in the attic began anew and continued, from time to time, throughout Chuck and Susan's tenure in the house.

The Aaron A. Sargent House

The charming Italianate Victorian at 449 Broad Street originated as a much smaller and much simpler two-story structure covered in redwood shiplap siding. It was built by Aaron Augustus Sargent sometime prior to 1865 for his new wife, Ellen, in that part of Nevada City which would later become known as "Nabob Hill." Over the years the house was expanded and renovated to, finally, become the house we see today.

Having arrived in Nevada City in 1850, Sargent started out as a writer for the *Nevada Daily Journal* and, sometime later, he became the newspaper's owner. By 1854 he had become a lawyer and, within two years, he was Nevada County's district attorney. Two years after that he turned to politics becoming, first, a California state senator, then a member of the United States House of Representatives and, finally, in 1873, a United States senator.

Ellen Clark Sargent was an early and fervent suffragette. Susan B. Anthony was a friend and houseguest of the Sargents and it was, no doubt, due to Ellen's influence that, in 1878, her husband presented to Congress the twenty-nine word bill which would, forty-two years later, become adopted as the Nineteenth Amendment to the United States Constitution, giving women the right to vote.

Sargent's record in the Senate, however, was not all so laudable as he was known as the "Senator for the Southern Pacific Railroad" and he was a fierce supporter of the Chinese Exclusion Act of 1882 as well as advocating for its extension in 1892; a notorious act of racial bigotry which would be indefinitely extended and remain "the law of the land" until 1943. He would later serve, for two years, as the United States' ambassador to Germany.

Although he was to end his days in San Francisco, it seems that both he and his wife may have returned in spirit form to their home on upper Broad Street. Not all that long ago, a lady told me that very early one morning, as she drove down Broad Street on her way to work, she was somewhat startled to see a man and a woman dressed in Victorian attire enjoying breakfast on the front porch of the Sargent House. She thought little of it at the time as people in Nevada City sometimes "dress up" in period clothing on special occasions. The next morning, however, as she again passed the house, she, again, saw the couple, again dressed in Victorian attire, enjoying their breakfast on the porch. Her curiosity aroused, he decided to take a second look through her rearview mirror. Upon doing so, both the Victorian couple and all of their breakfast paraphernalia had vanished.

The Charles E. Mulloy
House

The house about which I am most often asked is the stately Victorian situated within the "Y" where Broad Street splits into East Broad and West Broad Streets. Built in the late 1870's by Charles Mulloy, a wealthy and well respected businessman, the house would become the scene of a mysterious death.

On November 6, 1902, shortly after lunch, Mulloy announced that he would be going home early. When he failed to come to work the next morning, someone was sent to his house to check on him. Charles Mulloy was found hanging from a rope beneath a tree in the front yard. The death was ruled to be a suicide and strange things have been happening in his house ever since.

From 2002 to 2013, the house was owned by a couple who lived out of town and only frequented the house for short visits on an occasional basis. On one of their visits they complained of a window which flew open by itself no matter how often they attempted to keep it closed. In the end they prevailed over the troublesome window by screwing it shut.

During this time the neighbors often observed unaccountable phenomena to occur from within the unoccupied house. Smoke would sometimes be seen rising up from the chimney on a hot summer day when the house was vacant.

Then, one night, the neighbors summoned the police as lights could be seen turning on and off in the house. As the police had been given keys to the house to be used in case of an emergency, they quickly entered the house. After a thorough search, neither an intruder nor an explanation for the lights could be found.

On another occasion the fire department was called when a neighbor spotted smoke billowing out from one of the windows. Firemen rushed into the house but found neither smoke nor fire in the room from which the smoke had, only minutes before, been observed.

It was not long after the incident with the fire department that an acquaintance of mine who lived near the Mulloy House said to me, "I want to introduce you to one of my neighbors. He has a story about the Mulloy House you should hear." Upon meeting the gentleman in question, whose house on West Broad Street directly faces the western side of the Mulloy House, he said, "Mark, I don't believe in ghosts. I will never believe in ghosts. But there is something very strange going on in that house! No one is ever there but I sometimes see the shades going up and down in the windows. It starts at the front of the house and works its way to the back of the house."

One day, as he saw a shade go up in the window nearest the front of the house, he decided he would solve the mystery once and for all. He ran across the street and scaled the masonry on the side of the house until he was able to see through the window. No one was in the room but a large world globe on the floor was spinning round violently! He then checked all of the doors and assured himself that no one was inside the house.

In 2013 the house was sold to Barbara Ferrier and Fred Rudd, a delightful, retired married couple who, though knowing the house's history, have found it to be a completely wonderful house in which to live.

Barbara told me that she senses two ghosts in the house, Charles Mulloy and a lady whom she believes to be Charles' wife, Jessie. Barbara feels that Jessie, who was French Canadian, must have exerted some kind of psychic influence over her as, soon after having taken up residence in the house, she developed an unexpected and unexplainable interest in French music.

Several times during Barbara and Fred's first few months in the house a faucet handle in the downstairs half bath was turned by ghostly hands to the open position causing water to stream into the basin and requiring them to physically return the faucet handle back to the closed position each time.

Equally vexing issues were experienced by Barbara's niece who visited them for five days. First, a necklace of hers mysteriously vanished, only to reappear days later in her dirty clothes bag. Then, while showering in the upstairs guest bathroom just prior to her departure at the end of her visit, the water ceased flowing three times as she was washing her hair, necessitating her to turn the water back on each time. "Please let me finish washing my hair," she implored aloud, "I'll be leaving soon!" As if in answer, upon her turning on the water for the fourth time, the water remained on long enough for her to finish her shower.

A whiff of old-fashioned tobacco can sometimes be sensed in the upstairs master bathroom and their dog, Imus, has been known to intently watch an invisible presence.

The real-estate agent through whom they purchased the house told them that she often smelled the aroma of freshly baked cookies when she would open up the house in the morning. When, about three years ago, Barbara was entertaining guests, one of her guests inquired about the cookies she definitely smelled baking. Barbara had to explain that, sadly, it was only the scent of phantom cookies. Sometime later, the guest telephoned Barbara saying, "Your ghost must have come home with me for now I'm smelling the cookies in my house!"

One day Barbara heard a male voice shout, "Leave!" To this she firmly responded, "No, we like it here. You can leave if you wish but we're staying." And, now, aside from the occasional recalcitrant window which flies open refusing to stay shut, all is well in Nevada City's most asked-about haunted house.

The Charles E. Mulloy House today

East Broad Street

Yet another haunted house can be found on East Broad Street directly across the street from the old Pioneer Cemetery, a house which was built on what some believe to have originally been a part of the cemetery. A young lady who, years ago, lived in that house told me that she is convinced the house is haunted. The unexplainable strains of guitar music would sometimes issue from an upstairs room. The stereo was known to turn itself on without human assistance. Doors opened and closed by themselves and the individual rooms in the house would each exhibit differing degrees of temperature.

The Chinese Quarter

From the 1850's through the 1870's, the area along upper Commercial Street, starting from its convergence with Broad Street and continuing past York Street and on down to North Pine Street, was known as Nevada City's Chinese Quarter. Although the Chinese community featured a plethora of shops, a temple and services for almost everything from restaurants and laundries to barbers and brothels, very little of it remains today. Most of the wood framed buildings were destroyed when, in June of 1880, one of Nevada City's many fires swept through the Chinese community. Fortunately, at least three seemingly haunted buildings have survived.

At the corner of Commercial and York Streets, at 315 Commercial, is a building which was, at one time, a private residence and which was, at a later date, utilized as a storage place for flour used by a local bakery. The owner of a shop which once did business in this building told me that she would often think she saw someone or something moving in the store but, upon checking, would find that no one was there.

Next door you will find what once served as a Chinese grocery. Many years ago there was a hair salon in the building. Upon opening for business in the morning, the proprietor would often find a row of pennies on the floor. She would pick up the pennies and place them into her cash register. The next morning, however, she would, again, find the pennies back on the floor.

The building's next tenant was The Golden Flower Trading Company and Museum. Dix Sullivan, the shop's proprietor, told me that he sometimes felt the presence of the original Chinese grocer in his shop. He also said he would, at times, find the backdoor to be open although he had not noticed any customers having entered the shop from the Posh Nosh's outdoor dining area located between the back sides of the two buildings.

When I mentioned the hair stylist's strange experience with the reappearing pennies, Dix explained to me that Chinese shopkeepers would often hang, by the front door of their shop, an assemblage of Chinese coins tied together with a red ribbon or cord in order to insure prosperity. Dix had followed that tradition prior to opening The Golden Flower and, perhaps, this had relieved the ghost of the Chinese grocer of having to continually supply the "prosperity pennies."

When, years later, The Golden Flower had moved to Broad Street and another shop had moved into the building, I, one day, stopped by to ask the new shopkeeper if she had ever experienced anything strange in the shop.

"Yes," she answered, "I keep finding pennies on the step below my front door although I never see anyone leaving them there. I pick them up before closing and put them into the cash register. But, when I open up in the morning, there are the pennies again, inside the shop, on the floor in front of the door."

"I know how you can stop that," I said, suggesting that she hang a string of Chinese "wealth and success coins" by her front door.

"I did that when I first opened for business," she responded. "But a little boy played with them one day and made such a mess of it that I took the coins down." Upon reflection, she remembered that the pennies had not begun to appear until after she had removed the "good luck" coins.

In the years which followed I often heard from various tenants in the building of pennies mysteriously appearing on floor.

I also was to hear more accounts of the backdoor opening by itself, even after it had been securely locked for the night.

However, the ghost sometimes found itself compelled to close one or both of the shop doors. At one time a tenant of the building had a fractious relationship with the second owner of the Posh Nosh. When one afternoon the two headed towards each other in the outdoor dining area between the two buildings with what appeared to be less than amicable intentions, the backdoor violently slammed shut, followed, a few moments later, by the front door slamming shut as well.

On a more pleasant note, a young lady who worked in a different shop which once did business in the former Chinese grocery told me of how she had created a display of rings mounted with colored stones which was arranged in such a manner that the colors of the stones mimicked the pattern of a rainbow. Although she always made certain that the display was in perfect order when she closed up at night, upon arriving in the morning, she would often find that the rings had become rearranged into a random pattern.

Next door at 311 Commercial Street and currently serving as a one bedroom hotel suite is what, in the 1800's, had been a gambling parlor with a trapdoor in the floor which gave access to an opium den below.

At one time the building served as The Tanglewood Forrest, a unique shop selling items related to fairies, gnomes and elves. From time to time something would go missing in the store. The owner would, then, search everywhere for the missing item, all to no avail. The next morning, however, upon opening the shop, she would find the missing object set out before her in plain sight in a place where she knew she had carefully looked the day before. When I expressed interest in what I perceived to be ghostly phenomena, the shopkeeper retorted, "My shop isn't haunted."

"Then how do you explain items moving about the shop willy-nilly?" I asked.

"It's the fairies!" she responded with a perfectly straight face.

However, when, a few years later, a ladies' apparel shop moved into the old building, the new proprietor confirmed my suspicions, stating that she had similar experiences of merchandise moving about by itself in her shop. In particular, she recalled how, once, on a rainy day, she discovered that an article of clothing hanging on a rack was wet although no one had tried on the garment that day or, for any other reason, taken it outside the shop.

300 Commercial Street

When, years ago, the building at 300 Commercial Street housed the Country Rose restaurant, a woman in a white dress from the turn of the last century was often seen to pass by the window which looked out onto their outdoor dining area. The front door would open and close by itself and members of the restaurant staff reported sometimes feeling a ghostly presence. They would, on occasion, think they had heard patrons standing near the entrance waiting to be seated only to discover that no one was there. At times they would find themselves inexplicably stepping aside to let some unseen entity pass and, on one such occasion, the owner's daughter looked down to see a pair of disembodied shoes crossing the floor in front of her. One night, after the Country Rose was closed, while staff members were discussing the strange phenomena they so often encountered in the restaurant, the eerie sound of a woman's cackling laugh was heard to echo from within the room!

The owner, Michael Johns, told me that, while readying the restaurant for opening in the morning, he would sometimes see the ghostly woman in white reflected in the glass of the large framed graphics which, at the time, hung on one of the restaurant walls.

Matt Margulies, the next restaurateur to occupy the space told me that he saw the same woman while he was remodeling the building prior to opening his restaurant, Mateo's Public. Staff members at Mateo's often reported seeing the same ghostly lady in the vicinity of the restroom.

Around closing time, restaurant staff would sometimes hear voices just outside the restaurant speaking in a language which they thought might be Chinese although no one could be seen on the street at the time.

Friar Tuck's

Directly across to street, at 111 North Pine Street, is Friar Tuck's Restaurant and Bar. The original Friar Tuck's, which was established in 1973 and remained in business until it was destroyed by fire in March of 2002, was said to be haunted by a ghost they called "Murph." Light fixtures were known to swing back and forth without any discernible cause. Candles would be blown out for no apparent reason, a wind could be felt when there was no draft and disembodied voices were sometimes heard.

One day a chef observed a plate to shatter into bits without anyone handling it. On another occasion the owner, Greg Cook, was startled to see a silverware setup wrapped in a napkin fly off a table.

Upon reopening in May of 2003, Cook told a reporter for the *Grass Valley Union* that the fire had eliminated Murph. But fires rarely exorcize a ghost. Murph, it seems, had, perhaps, merely been getting accustomed to his new surroundings — biding his time and waiting to make his reappearance.

One night I was conversing with a party of diners at the new Friar Tuck's and, upon my mentioning Murph, we heard a nearby server scream followed by the unmistakable sound of crockery smashing violently into each other. "Something tore the dishes out of my hands!" the server exclaimed.

"Then Murph is back?" I asked.

"Yes," she quickly affirmed, "that happens a lot around here!"

The Doris Foley Library for Historical Research

The 1907 granite-faced Romanesque Revival style building at 211 North Pine Street, which in earlier days had been the Nevada City Library and now serves as Nevada County's historical research library, may very well house more than just books, old newspapers and other historical records. A librarian who once worked there told me of often having felt an unseen entity brush against her head and shoulders while carrying out her duties behind the vintage circulation desk and, when working alone at night down in the basement, of hearing the sound of someone walking across the floor above her.

Another lady told me that she always experienced a feeling of depression when working in the basement. She later learned that, sometime in the distant past, a man had committed suicide down there.

And, then, there is the strange, pungent odor reminiscent of urine which wafts from a particular spot where rare, old record books line the shelves.

237 Commercial Street

The gold rush era building at 237 Commercial Street was originally a saloon and it has been said that, at one time, a tunnel from its basement connected to one of Nevada City's many brothels so that patrons might visit said establishment in a discreet manner.

When, years ago, the building was home to a popular restaurant called Café Mekka, a lady in Victorian dress was said to be seen at times walking through the middle of the café heading towards one of the two front windows where she would then sit, appearing as if she were waiting for someone.

At one time Café Mekka encompassed both 237 and 239 Commercial Street. One day, Danielle, one of Mekka's employees, was startled to hear a loud noise coming from the portion of the restaurant at 239 Commercial Street. Upon investigation, she discovered that all of the ornate metal chairs which had been placed around one of the tables in that part of the building had rapidly and simultaneously been pulled a few feet away from the table.

Sometimes Danielle felt as if someone was passing closely by and she found herself stepping aside without her having any idea as to why she had done so.

Danielle and other employees also reported often getting what Danielle described as "weird" or "heavy" feelings when working in the back of the restaurant or in the storage area upstairs, an "I don't want to be there" feeling.

235 Commercial Street

While visiting Nevada City in May of 2021, Hector Lerma and some friends visited The Brick, a bar at 235 Commercial Street, and a ghostly figure appeared behind them in a photo which Hector took at the time. Although there have been no other reported sightings of the ghost, employees of The Brick have experienced instances of unexplainable phenomena which have convinced them that the bar is haunted.

Firehouse #1

Firehouse #1

Firehouse #1, erected in 1861, is, without a doubt, the most haunted building in Nevada City.

In 1947 the firehouse was taken over by the Nevada County Historical Society and converted into an historical museum. An early director of the museum, Dr. Hjalmer Berg, often spoke of hearing phantom footsteps when he was alone in the museum and of feeling areas of cold air in certain parts of the building.

The Historical Society president at the time, Rebecca Miller, reported a troublesome cabinet door which would fly open by itself. As fast as she could close the door, it would fly back open again. Finally, one day she had dealt with it long enough and sternly stated aloud, "Stop it! I don't have time for this!" At last the cabinet door stayed closed. She, then, heard footsteps walking away behind her but, when she turned around to see whoever it was that might have come into the building, she found no one was there — no one visible that is.

In desperation the museum staff put locks on the cabinet doors but, since that time, a lady in Victorian clothing has been seen searching through the cabinet, her hands effortlessly passing through the locked cabinet door.

A number of museum visitors have told of being pushed, shoved or tripped when standing near the Chinese altar which was saved from the Hou Wang temple which once stood in the Chinatown section of Grass Valley.

In the 1970's a well-known San Francisco Bay Area "psychic" was brought in to investigate. He claimed that two Chinese temple ghosts were protecting the altar, attempting to dissuade nonbelievers from getting too close to the sacred shrine. Although the psychic conducted an exorcism supposedly removing the ghosts, the phenomena around the altar continued unabated.

In 1987 Cheryl Swope, who visited the museum with her son, reported actually seeing the altar spirits. As she stood silently before the shrine, several Chinese men materialized before her. Some were kneeling while another man walked about slowly, his face bent low toward the floor. She blinked her eyes a few times and the figures vanished. She next heard a low, moaning sound and her son heard what he later described as chanting. As they turned to leave, an invisible force tripped or shoved her son, violently hurling him down onto the floor.

The haunted Hou Wang Temple altar

And then there was the day a visitor, having just climbed the staircase to the second floor, turned round and fled the Firehouse in terror screaming, "They're after me! They're after me!" No one was ever able to learn what had frightened her.

On yet another occasion, a Jesuit priest who, in the company of two university graduate students, had been viewing the exhibits upstairs, made his way back downstairs. "Is someone playing a joke on us?" he asked. After being assured by the museum representative that he had no idea as to what the visitor was referring, the priest reported having observed what he described as a heavy-set, "red-haired floozy" dressed in old fashioned clothing playing the organ on the second floor, an organ which, it was said at the time, had once graced one of Nevada City's ubiquitous bordellos.

Another retired museum director, Tony Smeaton, told me that he would often have to close the lid to the organ in order to prevent visitors from pressing down on its keys, only to find, upon opening up the next morning, the lid had, in the middle of the night, been pulled back out of the way.

One day he moved a red velvet upholstered piano stool (no longer on display) from its normal place at the organ to a new location in front of an antique sewing machine. The red-haired lady must have taken objection to the

The Organ played by the "Red-Haired Floozy"

move for, the next morning; Tony found that
the stool had been knocked over onto its side.
From that time on, Tony left the stool at its
preferred place by the organ.

Late one evening a Nevada city resident
happened to look up at the balcony of the
firehouse and was surprised to see that the
curtains behind the large windows in the
French doors leading onto the balcony were
moving although he knew that the museum
was closed at the time. He then saw, peeking
out from behind the curtain, a heavy-set
woman with what he called "Mercurochrome
red hair." The woman seemed so real to him
that, the next time he saw Tony, he remarked,
"If you are going to be entertaining women up
there after hours, they really should be more
discreet!"

In the late 1980's a woman visiting the
museum with her three to four-year-old
daughter, Sarah, while enjoying the exhibits
upstairs, became aware that her daughter was
no longer holding her hand. The lady turned to
look for Sarah and saw that the little girl was
attempting to talk to a tall man standing
nearby, hunched over a display case as if he
was trying to get a closer look at an item. As
Sarah continued in her attempt to engage the
man in conversation, he slowly turned and
looked at her with a countenance of such anger
and menace that the mother quickly pulled

Sarah away from him. Now feeling extremely uncomfortable, she said, "OK. We're going to go. We've seen enough," and hurriedly ushered her daughter down the staircase to the first floor.

As they started to exit the museum, the docent said, "As you're going to leave, I think I'll lock up and go to lunch."

"You're not going to lock up with the man still upstairs are you?" the mother asked.

At that the color drained from the docent's face and she started to shake saying, "There's no man upstairs. You've been my only guests all day."

"No, there is a man upstairs," the visitor insisted. "Maybe you somehow missed him when he came in." There was no mistaking what both she and her daughter had seen. The man was as solid and real as any living person.

"Here, hold my daughter's hand. I'll show you," she continued before running back up the staircase. Upon reaching the second floor, she found that the room was deserted and she experienced an intense chill she would never forget.

By the time she got back downstairs, the docent and her daughter were already standing on the sidewalk outside the museum. The docent was clearly upset and was still shaking as she locked the museum door. When they stepped back further from the building, they observed that the lace curtains behind the French doors were blowing from out of the room toward the street.

For many years to come Sarah would experience a reoccurring dream in which she would, again and again, find herself climbing the museum staircase and venturing on into the haunted second floor room.

On a more benign note, another apparition, whom one surprised visitor described as "a pleasant little old lady," has been observed sitting in a rocking chair upstairs. Some believe her to be Jennie Lee Rowe, whose photograph (as she had appeared in her prime) hangs on a wall near the French doors.

A young boy with dishwater blonde hair and smelling of Bay Rum and talcum powder, as if he had just come back from an old-fashioned barber, has been seen upstairs as well.

Ghostly activity has been so common at the museum that Tony said the ghosts were, in his words, "everyday normalcy." Quite often, at closing time, he would hear footsteps upstairs, sounding as if someone was heading toward the balcony, but, upon going upstairs to inform any stragglers that the museum was about to close, he would find the second floor to be completely deserted. Sometimes he would find the rocking chair, which at that time was situated in front of the French doors, slowly rocking back and forth as if to say, "Got you again, Tony!"

The haunted rocking chair

On another occasion, shortly after a man wearing a long trench coat had gone upstairs, both the docent in charge of the museum that day and another visitor who was viewing the exhibits downstairs heard the sound of the rocking chair rocking in a violent and rapid manner which reverberated loudly against the wooden floorboards above them. Immediately thereafter, the man in the trench coat fled down the staircase and hastily exited the museum. The docent and the other visitor rushed up the staircase to the second floor. The chair was still rocking with a vengeance. Surveying the strange scene, the docent quickly noticed that a small artifact which had been there earlier in the day was now missing. Could it be that one of the museum's ghosts had seen the man in the trench coat secrete the artifact under his coat and it had attempted to alert the docent to the theft by rocking the chair as noisily as possible?

Once, at closing time, Tony must have been momentarily possessed by one of the museum's ghosts as, without realizing what he was doing, he sat down in the rocking chair, immediately breaking a narrow green ribbon which had been stretched across its arms in order to prevent visitors from sitting in the chair. Upon realizing what he had done, Tony immediately rose from the rocking chair and started to tie the ribbon back together. However, realizing that the ribbon was looking a bit tattered, he decided to leave the broken ribbon as it was for the night and to replace it with a new ribbon the next day. Upon arriving back at the museum the next morning with the new ribbon, he was startled to find that unseen hands had neatly tied the broken ribbon back together again.

Finally, as if the resident ghosts are not enough, the museum houses a strange relic of what some claim to be "spirit photography." Hanging on a wall at the top of the staircase and dating to the 1880's, is a watercolor tinted photograph of a local Irish mine owner named Carrigan. To the right of Mr. Carrigan, the faint ghostly image of a young boy can be seen in the background. Upon seeing the printed photograph, it is said, Carrigan stated that he was thinking of his boyhood at the time the photograph was taken and he identified the image as being that of his much younger self. Or so the story goes.

I believe the photograph is a prime example of the kind of fraudulent, double exposure "spirit photography" which was all too often marketed to grief-stricken families from the mid-1800's through the early 1900's. However, you are encouraged to visit the museum and decide for yourself.

The Carrigan photograph

Haunted Grass Valley

Grass Valley's Beginnings

The story of Grass Valley began in 1849 when the first settlers, having crossed over the Sierra Nevada Mountains by way of Donner Pass, made camp near the intersection of the Steep Hollow Creek with the Bear River. Their cattle, being tired and hungry, wandered off looking for food and they were later found by the settlers grazing in a lush "grassy valley." This incident was to give the town which later sprung up there its name.

Settlers and miners gravitated to the area and, in October of 1851, Nevada City resident, Aaron Augustus Sargent, was to write:

"We can think of but one town of Upper California (San Jose) which will compare in pleasantness with Grass Valley. The dwellings among the trees, the gentle sway of the hills, the beautiful broad valleys, and the air mixed of primitiveness and business bustle, all go to make up a delightful spot.... The improvements taking place in Grass Valley are all of a solid nature: handsome houses are being erected, and stores with heavy stocks of goods are being prepared for the coming winter. There are many families already settled in the town, and more are coming, and when the pleasant, harmonizing influences of female society are more largely added to Grass Valley, the sun will not shine on a more desirable residence...."

As gold panning gave way to hardrock mining, large numbers of Cornish miners arrived to work in the labyrinth of mines which, today, lie beneath Grass Valley and they stayed to make up a significant portion of the town's population.

The Empire Mine Office

The Empire Mine

The Empire Mine, in operation from 1869 to 1956, is one of the oldest, deepest and richest gold mines in California, producing 5.8 million troy ounces of gold.

Now a California historic state park, there are many who claim that both the mineyard and the "Cottage" which mine owner, William Bowers Bourn Jr., had built from mine rock as a summer home are haunted.

A lady who, years ago, lived in Grass Valley wrote to me of how, in the late 1970's and in the early 1980's, she experienced, on at least three separate occasions, a scene of ghostly miners "who were scared, waiting to go to work down below. One time there were three fellows, another just one. They were considerably terrified and I witnessed this as if it were a very clear picture including some conversation of fear. There was conversation on one of the occasions about 'the cave in' the week before and not wanting to go at all but needing the money — some heavy fearful breathing, lots of mumbling, then finally cold silence as they went. I didn't see the men physically, just a bit of foggy like shapes. But I could see them in my mind, including clothing and gear, and the emotions were clear."

On one of these occasions she heard the sound of footsteps behind her as she stood there. She thought it was another tourist but, upon checking, no one was there.

Other visitors to the mine have spoken of hearing miners' voices and the sounds of long-gone equipment in the area of the mine shaft.

A man in old-fashioned clothing was once seen in the mine yard office at a time when no living person was present inside the building.

Docents working in the Cottage have spoken of creaking floorboards and cold drafts which defy any logical explanation and of feeling a ghostly presence in the house, perhaps, William Bourn Jr., himself; his wife, Agnes Moody Bourn; or, to my mind, more likely, Katie Moriarty, the Irish housekeeper and caretaker who, from the year 1900 until her retirement in 1943, ran the house with such supreme efficiency that she still found the time to bake cookies for the children in the Sisters of Mercy's Grass Valley orphanage.

It is said that the image of a woman in late Victoria or Edwardian clothing appeared in a photograph which was taken in the Cottage many years ago. Although, upon hearing of this, I tried to track down the photograph or to find someone who recalled actually seeing it, the photograph has yet to be found.

On June 29, 2021 I took several infrared photographs of the unoccupied Bourn Cottage. Although I saw nothing unusual at the time I took them, upon later examination of the photographs, I found what appears to be a face in the right-hand section of a second story window. Did I capture the image of a ghost or is it merely an optical artifact of some kind? The photograph is reproduced on the next page for your consideration.

Could it be the ghost of Katie Moriarty?

The Bourn Cottage

140

St. Joseph's Hall

St. Joseph's Hall

In 1863 Mother Mary Baptiste Russell and four other nuns of the Irish order, The Religious Sisters of Mercy, departed Ireland for Grass Valley where they were assigned to assist Father Thomas J. Dalton in the daily operations of St. Patrick's Church located at the end of South Church Street as well as to establish Saint Mary's Academy. Modeled along the lines of the Irish school system, it was open to all children ages six to fifteen.

The Sisters also soon found themselves taking in children orphaned due to mining accidents, illness or one of the many other dangers which made up a part of everyday life in Grass Valley at the time. As this was the only orphanage in Northern California, the Sisters of Mercy found themselves taking in orphans from as far north as Oregon and as far east as Nevada, swelling the convent by the 1890's to sixty nuns caring for four hundred orphans. The Holy Angels Orphanage at Mount St. Mary's continued to serve as the town's orphanage until the 1950's.

In 1894 the Sisters erected St Joseph's Hall, creating a complex which, today, is known as the St. Joseph's Cultural Center; a building now devoted to historical, artistic and cultural activities; a building which many believe to be haunted by at least one nun who may, perhaps, be none too pleased to see how the edifice they created for what they saw as the glory of God is now being utilized.

Years ago, when the Ghidotti Room was occupied by a belly dancing class, the door flew shut with a thunderous crash as if being slammed in anger by someone upset by dancers' scandalous gyrations!

On another occasion a young woman who was, at the time, waiting for a friend in the Bishop's Room felt herself grasped violently by the throat by an unseen entity as if it was attempting to choke her.

Shortly afterwards, her friend entered the room and, without knowing anything of the terrible experience she had just endured, he felt compelled to tell her about the ghost of a little girl said the haunt the upstairs areas of the building. So often has this spirit been seen that an artist who maintained a studio in the building had painted a portrait of her.

The little girl appears to be five or six years of age, has long flowing hair and is dressed in a white nightgown. Sometimes, rather than being seen, she is merely heard crying. The weeping always follows the same predictable pattern. First, she is heard gently crying but this soon turns into unrestrained, heart-rending sobbing which continues in intensity until the crying becomes mixed with a pathetic hiccupping-like sound, as if she is gasping for air; a sound not unlike that which one might produce if one were being choked.

A number of people have independently heard the ghostly sobbing. Marlene, a former docent with the building's Grass Valley History Museum, while closing the museum for the night, clearly heard the crying on two separate occasions and, thinking it was a child in distress, she followed the cries throughout the building, never succeeding in finding their source.

She kept her experience to herself but, sometime later, she was surprised when, one evening, an artist who had a studio at St. Joseph's asked her, "Marlene, does it bother you when you hear the little girl cry?" Pretending not to know to what the man was alluding, she asked him to explain.

One evening while playing a musical instrument, he had heard a little girl crying just outside his studio door. He opened the door only to find there was no one to be seen. The sobbing, however, continued from the invisible entity which seemed to be standing just outside his doorway.

"Please, little girl," he said. "Please don't cry. If you come in and stop crying, I will play a song for you." The sobbing stopped and he felt the entity enter into the room where it seemed to remain while he played a song for her.

That was only to be the first of several times upon which he heard the little girl cry. On one of these occasions, when he heard her crying outside his door, he invited her in promising, "If you come in and stop crying I will write a poem for you," and, again, the crying stopped as he proceeded to fulfill his promise.

Another of my informants told me of the time she toured the museum with her young son. The child became upset immediately upon entering the museum, claiming that they were being followed by a ghost. The mother, however, dismissed her son's complaint as being merely the product of an overactive imagination. When they entered a room which had been set up as a classroom would have looked in the 1800's, the boy pointed to a female mannequin dressed in an old-fashioned nun's habit and blurted out, "And the ghost looks just like her!"

A woman who ran a martial arts studio in the building told me that when she first began offering classes there she often heard the sound of children crying on the other side of a wall and, at times, she would see the dark shadow-like form of a woman emerge through the wall, float across the room and exit by passing through a locked door. After a few weeks, however, the sound of children crying gradually subsided until, finally, the crying ceased altogether.

A former director of the Cultural Center once spoke of the time she was carrying a heavy box down a steep staircase which terminates in the museum. She was wearing high heels and tripped on a stair. Just before she was about to experience what might have been a life-threatening fall down the staircase, however, an invisible presence grasped her by the shoulders and pulled her back to safety.

The Josiah Royce Branch Library

The Grass Valley Public Library at 207 Mill Street, erected in 1916 with funds from the Carnegie Endowment was named for the philosopher, historian and Harvard professor, Josiah Royce, who, in 1855, was born on the site upon which the library would later be built.

Whether it is ghosts from the time of Josiah Royce or it is spectral library patrons who occupy the main reading room after closing time is hard to say. But the old building does seem to take on a peculiar life of its own once the doors close at night to the general public.

A former children's librarian who would sometimes work in the children's room, situated in the library basement, long after the library had closed with the doors securely locked, told me of hearing the sound of footsteps echoing from the floor above her and other sounds suggesting that ghostly visitors may possibly take over the space once those bothersome flesh and blood patrons have departed.

The Del Oro Theatre

Having opened its doors on May 29, 1942, the Art Moderne style Del Oro Theatre is known to be haunted by numerous ghosts. There is the lady dressed in red who seems so substantial that a theater manager who saw her was unaware that she was a ghost until the figure effortlessly glided through a wall. And, then, there is the little girl thought to be, perhaps, ten years of age and dressed in clothing of an earlier era who is sometimes seen running down a hallway, in the company of a similarly clad young boy, where both of them disappear upon their passing through a wall.

A lady attired in a sparkling white dress has been observed standing up against the back wall of one of the building's three theaters. The lady in white is thought be a woman who, many years ago, fell to her death from either the theater roof or the fire escape. Some say she committed suicide while others say she was inebriated and accidentally fell. Others have claimed she was pushed to her death by her husband.

Another well known ghost is the man wearing an old-fashioned hat and heavy overcoat who has, from time to time, been viewed from one of the projection booths, sitting in one of the theaters below. The well known and highly respected local radio station personality, Tom Fitzsimmons, told me of the day on which, because it had begun to snow, he decided to drive his daughter home from her job at the theater. As he had arrived at the Del Oro long before the end of his daughter's shift, he decided to watch a movie while he waited for her to clock out. There was no one in that particular theater at the time he entered it but, shortly before the film began, a man entered the theater, walked past Tom's row and sat down a few rows behind him. There was no possible way the man could have gotten up and left the theater without Tom seeing him do so but, when the lights came up at the end of the film, the man had vanished. When Tom asked his daughter, who had a clear view of the exit door, if she had seen the man leave, she answered, "No one entered or left the theater after you had gone in." As Tom put it, "In the side theatre at the Del Oro, there is no way someone could exit and not be noticed. I even walked up to the top of the theatre seats to see if the gentleman was there and there was no one."

Projection booth number two has a particularly ominous reputation. An employee once heard someone call out to him from the booth although no one was in the booth at the time and another employee steadfastly refused to ever enter into that booth alone. In the days prior to digital projection, a projector would, from time to time, turn on all by itself and large film cans were known to fly off the shelves.

The sound of someone walking on the stage in front of the main screen has been heard when no one is there. One night, after all of the customers had departed, the theater staff decide to try to contact the ghosts. Having assembled on the stage, they brought out a Ouija board and asked for any spirits present to make themselves known. No sooner had they done so than they clearly heard the footsteps of an invisible presence making its way down an aisle towards them. That was all the otherworldly contact they desired to experience that night and they immediately ended the session.

It was around that same time that two employees who had entered the no longer used and normally locked boiler room were startled to see a colored light emerge from within a wall and rush towards them.

Locked doors are said to open and close by themselves and lights are known to be switched on and off by unseen hands. One day an employee became so frustrated by the continual ghostly phenomena that he began screaming at whatever ghost might be responsible. As if in retaliation, the water fountain shot out a spray of water in his direction.

More recently a scratching sound was heard coming from a hallway. When staff members investigated, they found fresh scratch marks on the wall near a locked closet. Upon opening the closet, they found a vintage locket lying on the floor; a locket which had not been there before.

However, perhaps the strangest and most baffling of all the inexplicable events to have occurred at the Del Oro occurred during the course of two of my Haunted Grass Valley tours. Two weeks before Halloween, as I was in the middle relating stories involving the Del Oro's ghosts, a deluge of popcorn began to fall from the sky, quickly covering the sidewalk in front of the ticket booth. While many on the tour took it to be an example of ghostly intervention, I felt certain it was a Halloween season prank perpetrated by a Del Oro employee hiding up on the theater roof and I said so at the time. After all, the staff knew that I always came by with a tour at that time in the evening on Friday nights in October and I was convinced that they had conspired to play a practical joke.

Upon the completion of the tour, I circled back to the Del Oro where some of the employees were preparing to close the theater. "All right," I laughed, "which one of you jokers threw the popcorn from the roof during my tour tonight?" They all denied having anything to do with it and added that it would have been impossible for any of them to have done so as, following the death of the woman who had fallen from the roof years before, the door opening onto the roof was always kept securely locked and the manager was the only one who had the key.

At that precise moment the manager came outside. She had heard us talking about the popcorn and she entered into the conversation. She had seen the popcorn on the sidewalk earlier and had thought one or more of the theater's customers had been responsible for the mess which she, herself, had to sweep up from the pavement. She produced the ring of theater keys from her pocket and stated, in no uncertain terms, that the roof had been locked all night and that she had the keys in her possession throughout the entire evening.

A few nights later I had a private tour and, as all of the guests were staying at the Holbrooke Hotel and, as we had a late start, I decided to conduct the tour backwards, beginning at the Holbrooke, and we eventually worked our way down to the Del Oro well over an hour later. As I was finishing telling the stories about the Del Oro, the manager happened to join us outside.

"No one is going to believe me if I tell them what happened last Friday night" I said to her. "Would you tell them about it?"

No sooner had she begun to tell the story than it happened again. Only this time it was not popcorn but small torn up pieces of the napkins dispensed at the theater's concession stand which softly fell from the sky upon us like snow. We all ran out into the street in an attempt to see anything which might account for what was happening. After the flurry of torn paper, including a piece which had been tied together in the shape of a ring, finally ended, two members of our group stated that they had clearly seen a little girl standing at the edge of the roof laughing as the bits of paper floated down upon us.

As no one could have possible known that I would be bringing a tour group by that evening, much less that late in the evening, I cannot believe that what we experienced that night could possibly have been a prank of any kind. To this day it remains, for me, a never to be solved mystery.

The Owl Tavern

The building at 134 Mill Street which for generations served as The Owl Tavern is actually make up of two buildings dating to 1857 and 1862. The Owl became a saloon in 1883 earning its name back in the days when, as the gold mines operated twenty-four hours a day, the saloon stayed open at all hours in order to offer liquid relief to parched and exhausted miners.

During those years The Owl was believed to have been haunted by as many as a dozen ghosts who made life extremely difficult for waitresses who were constantly harassed by mischievous phantom hands which untied their aprons, pinched them and engaged in other inappropriate physical behavior causing them to consider seeking employment elsewhere. How they managed to count the ghosts and determine their exact number was not recorded. What was recorded, however, is that the problem became so unendurable that, finally, a priest was called from St. Patrick's Church and asked to conduct an exorcism. The exorcism apparently proved successful as the ghostly harassment of waitresses ceased, at least for the time being. I say "for the time being" as at least one ghost has stubbornly refused to leave and, only a few years, ago a young lady tending bar at The Owl told me that she sometimes felt an invisible hand on her back or shoulder and that her apron would, at times, inexplicably become untied.

The Owl's most famous ghost, whom they call "George," presides over what is often called the "Haunted Booth," the booth situated in the left-hand corner of the back of the building. Servers at The Owl often told diners sitting in that booth to employ the old football cheer, "Push 'em back! Push 'em back! Push 'em way back!" This was because the ghost was notorious for sliding items off the table and into diners' laps.

A typical experience was that related to me by a woman who, along with her husband, had, years ago, dined at The Owl while seated in the Haunted Booth. For no apparent reason her fork kept falling off the table. When, at the end of their meal, she got up to leave, she found a spoon had, somehow, made its way into her purse.

After learning from the bartender of the booth's reputation, the couple returned to The Owl on another occasion and asked to, again, be seated in the Haunted Booth where they were joined by the lady's brother. When they told the brother the story of their previous experience, he scoffed at very thought of the booth being haunted. As if in answer to a challenge, a bottle of wine immediately slid across the table. Once the bottle came to a stop, the trio carefully examined both the bottle and the table top, thinking that, perhaps, moisture had caused the bottle to slide. Both the bottom of the bottle and the table were bone dry.

A former bartender told me of how, late one night, as he was preparing to close up, upon passing the Haunted Booth, he observed a knife and spoon to fly off the table and up into the air towards him.

The explanation for the ghostly behavior may lie in Grass Valley's often turbulent past. There was a time when gambling took place at The Owl and a man playing cards where the Haunted Booth is now located is said to have been caught cheating. He was summarily shot dead where he sat.

Ghostly activity at The Owl is not, however, confined to the Haunted Booth. One night, just prior to closing, a bartender saw what he described as "a black something" appear behind the bar, pass through the bar, turn to the right and continue on, gliding toward the back of the building.

A former owner of The Owl had a habit of tapping on the upholstery of each of the three booths in the back section of the restaurant as he headed toward the back door and home at the end of each evening. One night, upon making his customary tap on the first booth, his tap was followed, as if in answer, by a disconcerting second tap. When he tapped on the second booth, the tap was, again, repeated. The same thing occurred when he tapped on the third booth as well.

The 1800's style swinging saloon doors in the hallway leading to the restrooms have been observed to swing back and forth at times when no one has recently passed through them.

An employee once found herself trapped in the lady's restroom. As she vainly attempted to turn the doorknob, she found it refused to budge. She seemed to be struggling with someone far stronger than herself on the other side of the door who insisted on turning the knob in the opposite direction.

One night as we approached The Owl on my Haunted Grass Valley tour, a gentleman told me that his young son needed to use a restroom. He decided to take his son into The Owl and said they would catch up with us later. Although he had not heard any of my stories about The Owl, when, quite a while later, he and his son returned to the tour, the father exclaimed, "You won't believe what happened. We couldn't get out of the men's room. I couldn't get the doorknob to turn!"

And then there was the night an employee was asked to close up after counting the money in the cash register. After placing the currency out onto the bar, she remembered that she needed to tend to a task down in the basement. While downstairs, she clearly heard the sound of footsteps directly above her in the now locked and unoccupied bar. Completely unnerved, she fled the building in terror and telephoned the owner from her home. "Your money is on the bar," she informed him. "If you want it put away, you need to come down and do it yourself. I'm not coming back!"

Chinatown

Grass Valley's Chinatown once flourished in the area where the Miner's Inn hotel is presently located. From 1860 to 1880 the Chinese, lured by tales of what they called "Gold Mountain," emigrated to Grass Valley, creating a vibrant community, which until it was destroyed by fire in 1877 and its last remnants obliterated in 1938, was second only to San Francisco in population and featured such amenities as stores, gardens, opium dens and what were blissfully referred to as "houses of joy."

During the years between the demise of the Chinatown and the construction of the hotel, this location was home to, among other things, an appliance store, a bowling alley, an office building and Nelda Honey's dance studio. And it is upon Nelda Honey, who tirelessly taught ballet, tap dance and other forms of dance to generations of aspiring young dancers, that we shall now focus.

One of Nelda's passions was local theatre and, in the 1980's, she converted a warehouse adjacent to her dance studio into an intimate ninety-nine seat theater which she christened, The Studio Theatre. Considering the many years she personally financed scores of theatrical productions and made numerous other monetary sacrifices in order to keep the doors open, it would not be at all surprising if, following her death, she might have felt completely justified in refusing to leave the theater which she, almost single-handedly, had built. And it is quite possible that this is exactly what occurred.

In the years following Nelda's passing, the Studio Theatre was leased by a local community theatre group. During this time, the theater manager, Margot Malone, told me she often felt Nelda's presence in the building and, each morning, as she entered the theater, she would say, "Hi, Nelda." It came as no surprise to her when, one day, upon doing so, she heard Nelda's deep and highly distinctive voice respond with a cheerful, "Hi!"

As Nelda has not been heard from since the time of the Studio Theatre's demolition, it is assumed that she finally decided it was time for her to pass on to her justly deserved reward on "the other side."

The Ghost Train

Not far from what had once been Grass Valley's Chinatown, in an area on Bennett Street bounded by Bank Street to the west and Kidder Avenue to the east, there once stood the Grass Valley depot for the Nevada County Narrow Gauge Railroad. As the railroad, which began operation in 1876, only traveled the 22.53 miles from Colfax to Grass Valley to Nevada City and back again and its rolling stock was emblazoned with the initials, N.C.N.G.R.R., the railroad was often referred to by the locals as the "Never Come Never Go Railroad."

In 1942 the railroad ceased operation. Its rails were torn up to be melted down to make armaments for the Second World War and its rolling stock was scrapped or sold off. One of the locomotives, #5, the Tahoe, however, had a second life in Hollywood motion pictures before finally returning to Nevada City where it now resides in the Nevada County Narrow Gauge Railroad Museum.

A woman who, as a child, had lived in the vicinity of Grass Valley depot told me that, although she knew it was impossible, she often heard the unmistakable sound of a train passing through her neighborhood. When she finally mentioned hearing it to a friend, the friend responded, "That's the 'ghost train.' We all hear it."

I was ready to dismiss the "ghost train" as being merely a misinterpretation of natural, fully explainable ambient sounds until she told me of the day when, years later, she clearly saw, standing upon what remains of the passenger entrance to the Grass Valley depot, a lady dressed in old-fashioned clothing, a vintage suitcase by her side. The lady with the suitcase turned and, upon realizing that she had been seen, immediately melted away into nothingness.

Bennett and Bank Streets where the vanishing lady was seen standing upon what remains of the depot's passenger entrance.

A Haunted Miner's Cabin

Nearby, a converted miner's cabin on Depot Street is haunted by what appears to be a miner in his forties. Wearing a plaid shirt and shod in brown work boots, he has often been seen loitering in the hallway or sitting in a chair which he has been known to move about to suit his mood. Even during those times when he is not to be seen in his favorite chair, the ever cautious house cat will give the chair a wide berth, circling far around it. On one occasion, the ghostly miner annoyed the lady of the house by moving some dining utensils she had just finished washing and which she had laid out to dry.

111 Mill Street

In the 1920's this building was occupied by Gil Miller, the town's undertaker, and that may well account for the strange occurrences which have been reported in the basement where he prepared his "clients" for burial. At one time there was said to have been a rectangular opening in the front of the building covered by a hinged flat, similar to the night book return at a library, through which corpses could be conveniently dropped off if the establishment happened to be closed at the time. Due to the consistently cool year-round temperature of the basement, it also has been said that the basement was used for a time as the town morgue.

Previous tenants speak of the basement in hushed tones, confessing that they tried to not go down into the basement any more often than was absolutely necessary. An eerie whistling sound could sometimes be heard down there. On other occasions, strains of music and happy voices could be heard along with the clinking of glasses, as if engaging in ghostly toasting, along with the sound of glasses or bottles being tapped onto the surface of a table or a bar, perhaps spectral echoes of the time when the basement served as a barroom.

Once, when a previous storekeeper went down into her storage area in the back portion of the basement, she unexpectedly heard the basement door close by itself behind her, quickly followed by the chilling click of the lock on the other side of the door, trapping her alone in the haunted basement until her frantic pounding on the door and cries for help alerted a passerby to her plight.

116 Mill Street

This building, built in 1855 and currently occupied by Yuba Blue, was, for decades, the home of Grass Valley Hardware, and it was here, on the second floor, that the *Grass Valley Union* first began publication. A woman with long flowing blonde hair has been seen floating through the store at night while a former employee told me of seeing a figure clad in a hooded robe in the building, of having seen merchandise move about by itself and of occasionally seeing a dark fog-like "something" roll across the floor in the early morning hours.

The Odd Fellows Hall

Situated on the second floor above the Old Town Café at 110 Mill Street (its entrance being at back of the building at 113 South Church Street) is the Odd Fellows Hall. A ghostly figure dressed in Odd Fellows regalia of a bygone era has been seen in their ceremonial chamber.

104,106 and 108 Mill Street

The large building which houses businesses at 104, 106 and 108 Mill Street clearly hides within its walls more than its fair share of secrets. Many years ago, when a wine shop did business at 108 Mill Street, the proprietor was surprised, late one night, to hear the sound of piano music issuing from the second floor directly above him, a space which, at the time was untenanted and completely empty. Not long after that a shopkeeper at 104 Mill Street told me of hearing the same music and the sound of people dancing coming from the same empty space above her shop. Years later, a member of the Odd Fellows told me that he often heard, through the wall between the two adjoining buildings, the unmistakable sounds of someone moving about in the unused second floor above the three shops comprising 104, 106 and 108 Mill Street. Each of these instances of ghostly sounds emanating from within the unoccupied second floor was experienced independently with none of the three witnesses having been aware of what any of the other witnesses had experienced. The early history of the building provides an explanation. At one time the upstairs featured a ballroom called The Music Room.

The ghosts do not, however, confine their activities to the second floor. An unexplainable coldness is sometimes felt at 108 Mill Street when one passes beyond the iron doors at the back of the shop and those who have worked in the building in the past tell of objects moving by themselves, of items exploding, and of pictures and merchandise flying from shelves and off the walls. A former 108 Mill Street tenant told me that, on more than one occasion, upon arriving at her shop, neighboring Mill Street merchants told her of having heard gunshots coming from the back of her shop earlier that morning. Upon investigating the building's history, she discovered that, back in the days of Grass Valley's often violent past, a man had been shot to death in the area behind the iron doors at the back of the building.

And then there was the evening the owner of an antiques shop then doing business at 206 Mill Street discovered to his dismay that, as a heavy rain pelted down upon the building, water was leaking through the ceiling from the floor above him. He and an employee ran up to the second floor where they hastily arranged tarps in such a manner as to channel the water seeping in from the roof into buckets. After trying this for around forty-five minutes, however, the buckets had already become half full. Realizing that their efforts were futile, they reluctantly gave up for the night and went home. The next morning they made their way back upstairs expecting the worse. To their amazement, they found that all of the buckets were empty and the floor was completely dry!

One day a customer at the antiques shop was startled to see a cabinet drawer open by itself. "How did you do that?" the lady asked the store owner.

"I didn't do it," the proprietor responded.

"Of course you did it!" the customer retorted. "Tell me how you did it!"

"I didn't do it," he vainly tried to explain.

Absolutely convinced that the shopkeeper was perpetrating some kind of practical joke, the highly disgruntled customer called the shopkeeper an extremely vulgar name and left the shop in a huff.

107 Mill Street

Books have been known to fall from their shelves from time to time at The Book Seller at 107 Mill Street and, one day, one of their tall circular display stands mysteriously toppled over. These occurrences could be assumed to have "natural" explanations if it were not for the time a young girl told me of her having seen a book slide by itself along a flat and level surface in the bookstore's children's section downstairs.

102 Mill Street

The building at 102 Mill Street, built in 1854 for the Adams Express and Stage Company, was Grass Valley's first brick building. Having been utilized by the *Grass Valley Union* in the 1870's and, then, later as a grocery and a clothing store, in the early 2000's the upstairs was, for many years, the home of a hair salon called The Flying Hare.

Around two in the morning while Rachel Kelly, the owner of The Flying Hare, and her son were at work remodeling the upstairs in preparation for opening the salon, they were surprised to hear a woman singing in a lilting, ethereal, otherworldly voice. Although they felt the voice had definitely come from inside the room, they quickly checked to see if there was anyone outside on the street who could account for the ghostly singing. The streets were completely empty.

It was during this period of remodeling that, one day, Rachel's son used the shower in the salon's bathroom and, after doing so, told his mother that he did not ever want to use that shower again as he felt that the bathroom was haunted. Although he had not heard or seen anything out of the ordinary, he could not shake the feeling of having shared the room with an unseen presence.

Sometime later, after the remodeling had been completed and the salon had opened for business, a client used the facilities and, upon emerging from the restroom, she also declared that the room was haunted. The client was so struck by the experience that she took it upon herself to do some research and discovered that, sometime in the past, a little girl had drowned in a bathtub in that room.

Things came to a head when Rachel commissioned a young woman to paint a mural on one of the shop's walls. As the artist had previously arranged to depart in two days time for a trip to South America and needed to complete the mural before she left, she decided to work as long into the evening as possible and to spend the remainder of the night sleeping in the building.

Sleep, however, was not to be hers. That night she was awakened by the ghost of a little girl who said her name was Jamie and who asked the artist to stay awake with her. Several times during the course of the night the artist found herself nodding off only to be awakened each time by the little girl who would cry out in an imploring voice, "Wake up! Wake up! Please stay awake with me."

When, years later, The Flying Hare closed its doors, the second story of the building was, for a time, occupied by the Security Gold Exchange. As an informant had told me that, during the remodeling of the space for its new occupant, a carpenter had seen the form of a lady in old-fashioned clothes float across the room, I decided to ask the new proprietor if he had experienced anything unusual in the space.

"No, nothing unusual has happened up here," he replied. However, upon my inquiring further, he disclosed that, although he always turned out the light in the stairwell and turned the sign hanging behind a window in the street level door to read "Closed" when he locked the door at night, often, upon coming back in the morning, he found that the light in the stairwell was on or that the sign on the door had been turned back around to read "Open."

Could it be that Jamie had turned on the light and turned the sign to read "Open" in the hope of luring in someone to keep her company at night?

The Hardscrabble Building

Some authorities state that the Hardscrabble Building at 107 West Main was erected in the late 1850's for the firm of Harris and Saxon, furniture dealers. Another source, however, claims it was built for an undertaker who not only tended to the needs of the dead there but, also, built his own coffins in the back part of the building. And it is quite possible that both accounts are correct as furniture makers in those days were often known to make coffins as well.

Vague rumors have long circulated suggesting that the building is haunted. As night descends upon Grass Valley, it has been claimed that a strange fog-like substance can sometimes be seen to slowly materialize and grow in size until, at last, it passes through the door and into the building where it lingers for some time before, later that evening, passing back through the locked door and out into the street.

According to another, perhaps, apocryphal tale, the undertaker often displayed his coffins in the front window of the building. One day, it is claimed, he was surprised and, no doubt, more than a bit perplexed to have a passerby stop in to ask who it was that was lying so serenely in one of the coffins in the window — a rather difficult question to answer as all of his "clients" were, at the time, either reposing in what served as a viewing room or waiting in the preparation room in the back!

A more recent occupant of the building who sold ladies' apparel told me that articles of clothing would often be found to have mysteriously moved about in her shop and the unmistakable clicking sound of coat hangers being moved along a clothes rack would sometimes be heard when she was alone in the store.

The Washington Brewery Building

Depending upon which source you might choose to consult, the Washington Brewery Building at 114-116 East Main Street was built in either 1858 or 1862 and served as a brewery until it was closed during the years of Prohibition. At some point in its history the upstairs was converted into apartments. A young lady living with her daughter in one of those apartments went through a ritual each night in which, after tucking her daughter into bed, she would pretend to chase the ghosts and other imaginary monsters from her little girl's room before her daughter went to sleep. This nightly ritual took on a surprising seriousness late one night, however, when the young lady saw the vapor-like apparition of a woman at the end of her hallway. The ghost, she told me, was very much like a shadow only the reverse in color — light where a shadow would be dark.

The Alpha Building

The Alpha Building at 204 West Main, built of local mine rock in the 1870's as Peter Purcell's Fashion Livery Stable, was later known for generations as the Alpha Hardware Building. After Alpha Hardware closed its doors for the last time, the building was, for some years, home to a Goodwill Thrift Store. During that time the building was said to be haunted by a ghost the staff called "Casper" because he was, by and large, a friendly ghost.

On one occasion approximately twenty pictures of varying sizes were displayed for sale by hanging them from a line which stretched across the width of the building. At the end of the day, the store was locked for the night as usual. The next morning, when the staff opened up for business, they were startled to find that all of the pictures were now hanging upside-down!

Not all of Casper's manifestations, however, were quite so playful. He was believed to harbor a particular dislike for one specific assistant manager. One day, while she was in the stock room in the back of the building,

Casper grasped her pony tail and yanked on it so violently that she immediately tendered her resignation.

Sometime later a lady named Sandy became the store manager and it was during her tenure that one night a severe storm caused one or more signs in the store to blow down setting off the burglar alarm. Sandy was awakened in the middle of the night by the police who requested that she to go down to the store to turn off the alarm and to let them in so that they might look around and make certain that nothing was amiss. Throwing on a bathrobe, she quickly arrived at the store. The police searched the building and, once certain that there were no intruders, the police departed, Sandy locking the door behind them. Immediately thereafter, she set down her keys on a table near the door. When she, herself, was ready to leave, however, her keys were no longer where she was certain she had left them. She carefully searched the entire store looking for the keys but all to no avail. By now it was five-thirty in the morning and, as she needed to go back home in order to dress more appropriately for business, she was becoming frantic. In desperation, she called out, "Casper, if you don't want me to be fired, you need to find my keys for me." Immediately upon doing so, Sandy looked down and found the keys to be lying on the floor directly in front of her feet.

126 West Main Street

The building at 126 West Main Street once served as a bar and it is surmised that, perhaps, the ghost who haunts the building is a former barman or patron who objected to his former "home away from home" being taken over by a purveyor of ladies clothing when, back in the early 2000's, it was transformed into Vanity Faire Hats & Ladies Finery. A lady working there told me of being brushed on the back by an unseen presence, of lights turning on and off by themselves and of objects which were set down in one place being later found in an entirely different location. On one occasion a large armoire toppled over, having violently thrown itself forward onto the floor!

The Holbrooke Hotel

The Holbrooke Hotel at 212 West Main Street, if considered in terms of ghosts per square feet, may possibly be the most haunted hotel in the entire world.

Established in the year 1855 as the Exchange Hotel and renamed the Holbrooke Hotel after it was bought in 1870 by Ellen and Daniel Holbrooke, the Holbrooke has played host to four presidents of the United States, Grover Cleveland, James Garfield, Ulysses S. Grant and Benjamin Harrison, as well as to such colorful personalities as the writers, Mark

Twain and Bret Harte, the heavyweight championship boxer, Gentleman Jim Corbett, the dancer and "adventuress," Lola Montez, and Charles E. Boles, the dapper and elusive stagecoach bandit known as Black Bart.

But it is the unregistered guests with whom we are concerned; restless spirits who refuse to leave this unique relic of a bygone era, saturating its rooms and hallways with their undeniable presence,

Its Golden Gate Saloon, believed to be the oldest continuously operated saloon west of the Mississippi, has often been the scene of inexplicable events. Late at night when the saloon is closed and hotel guests are asleep in their rooms, the voices of a crowd from another era can sometimes be heard issuing from within the saloon. Curious smoke-like clouds have been observed rising toward the ceiling and a former employee told me of the time when, around eleven at night, all of the wine glasses suddenly began to shake frantically.

Parapsychologists, scientists who study such things, tell us that incidents from the past, particularly violent or highly emotional events, may sometimes imprint themselves into the walls, floors, ceilings and furnishings of the rooms in which such incidents have occurred, becoming an indelible part of the atmosphere — psychic imprints replaying themselves over and over again, unnoticed by all but those blessed, or should I say cursed, by the ability to see and hear these ghostly echoes of the past.

But such an explanation could hardly account for the disturbing incident experienced by the desk clerk who, one night, thought he might catch up on his sleep for a few hours on the couch in what, prior to the recent renovation of the hotel, was called the Library, a room adjacent to and separate from the saloon. Having fallen asleep, he was startled to find himself rudely awakened by lights shining in the empty, locked and previously darkened saloon. When he arose and walked toward the bar to investigate, the lights went out. He then waited and watched in disbelief as, a few minutes later, the lights came back up again.

But such ghostly phenomena do not occur only in the small hours of the night. Consider the case of the bewildered young boy who, not all that long ago, complained to his parents of excessively loud voices coming from the Library; a room which was, upon examination, unoccupied.

Such events are not at all unusual at the Holbrooke. Back in the days when the reception desk was located across from the Library, from time to time, members of the hotel staff reported seeing the image of a man from another era sitting behind the desk, an image which would, then, quickly vanish.

The vintage elevator has often been known to move from floor to floor late at night when all of the hotel's guests are fast asleep, its door opening to reveal no one inside.

Eleanor Kenitzer, who served for many years as the Holbrooke's manager, told me of how, one day, a tray of silverware and napkins was knocked out of her hands by unseen forces as she passed from the kitchen toward the reception desk; an event which was to be experienced again, over a decade later, in exactly the same way and in exactly the same place, by a restaurant server.

But the incident with the tray was not all that unique for Eleanor who had experienced an unusual array of paranormal events from her vantage point behind the reception desk looking out onto an area where ghosts were known to move chairs about and turn the lights on and off.

It was, also, not at all unusual for the telephone indicator lights at the reception desk to flick on when no one was on the other end of the line or for the calculator or the computer at the front desk to operate by themselves.

One day Eleanor noticed someone standing on the landing situated midway up the staircase leading to the second floor. The figure stood there for a long period of time, perhaps as long as five minutes. Eleanor kept looking up from time to time to see if the guest was still there. When another employee noticed this and asked, "What are you looking at, Eleanor?" she explained that she was curious as to why the guest was lingering so long there on the landing.

"There's no one there," the baffled employee answered.

"Don't you see him?" Eleanor responded in disbelief.

"No," the employee repeated.

And then there was the evening when the entire hotel appeared to be under assault. A violent pounding was heard on each of the Holbrooke's windows; an ominous rapping which began at the front entrance and, then, raced round the entire building. Although hotel staff rushed out to apprehend whoever might have been perpetrating a prank, no flesh and blood prankster was ever discovered.

In the North Star Hall, which once served as the hotel's dining room, there was, at that time, close to the entrance, a booth known as Table 15 where, from time to time, a member of the wait staff would observe a rather uniquely dressed couple to be sitting but, when the server returned to take their order, the couple was always found to have vanished. The gentleman who sometimes would initially be seen sitting alone reading a newspaper was dressed in a Victorian morning suit and top hat while the lady, who would later join him at the table, wore a Victorian dress complete with a bustle.

The man in the top hat has also been seen mingling with guests at weddings and parties, always fitting in and never causing the slightest problem, unless of course, he should be seen to unexpectedly vanish before their eyes.

Even when the phantom couple was not to be seen at Table 15, patrons sitting on the side of the booth favored by the Victorian couple would often quickly find themselves moving to the other side of the booth although they couldn't explain why they had felt compelled to do so. Other patrons have reported feeling a "cold spot" where Table 15 used to be, a sensation of dizziness, the fear that they are about to fall down or experiencing the hair on their arms or at the back of their neck to stand on end.

One night, as I was telling a tour group about Table 15, a guest with a toddler in a stroller cried out, "Mark, you have to see this!" Every hair on her daughter's head was standing on end as if she had been shocked by a static electricity generator.

Just beyond where Table 15 once was and through a doorway is the kitchen where an undefined "something" has all too often been encountered. Mischievous spirits have been known to fling culinary utensils from the racks upon which they had been hanging and the water taps have been repeatedly turned on by unseen hands.

Those who study such things have an explanation for such events, a phenomenon which they term "poltergeist," a German word meaning "noisy ghost." They suggest that such events are due not to ghosts at all but are due, instead, to unconscious and uncontrollable psychokinetic energy thought to be flowing from an adolescent experiencing a period of extreme emotional stress. But this theory could hardly account for phenomena occurring in a hotel which is staffed entirely by adults. Nor could it explain the experience of the staff member who, one day, while approaching the kitchen's walk-in freezer, felt a ghostly "something" tap him on the shoulder.

And what of those spirits who seem possessed of a demonstrable consciousness, clearly seeming to interact with the living; spirits whose actions suggest the survival of individual, personal consciousness past death; spirits whose actions may, just possibly, help answer the question which has haunted mankind for millennia; the question which haunts our hearts and minds, that most important of all questions. What happens to us when we die and our bodies are returned to the welcoming embrace of the earth?

The ghosts of the Holbrooke range in age from the sedately mature to ghost children who have frequently been heard running up and down the upstairs hallways laughing and giggling. The children can sometimes be heard playing inside an unoccupied room, particularly Rooms 15, 16 and 17, jumping up and down on the bed.

If, however, their favorite rooms have been booked, they usually confine their playing to the hallways. Many a guest has called down to the desk in the middle of the night requesting that something be done about the noise caused by the children in the hallway, a request with which it is impossible for the hotel staff to comply. However, each time such a complaint has been lodged, the children seem to know and quiet down of their own accord. All in all, they are quite well behaved for ghost children, and, most of the time, only the faint murmur of childish voices can be heard to waft down the hallways, echoing a time of youthful innocence.

A few years ago, during the course of a tour, a lady mentioned that, on a previous visit to the Holbrooke, her approximately five-year-old daughter had told her that she had seen children of her own age, whom she called her "friends," playing in the hotel's basement. However that night she stated that her friends were upstairs on the second floor. Having informed the other members of the tour as to the child's claim, I decided to try an experiment, asking the child to lead us to her friends. The little girl quickly ran up the staircase, turned right and led us directly to Room 17. "They're in there," she declared while pointing to the door; Room 17 being one of the three rooms in which the ghost children have been known to play.

In 2010 I was asked to appear in an episode of the television program, *My Ghost Story*, concerning an intriguing photograph which had been taken at the Holbrooke.

Mary Moore and her husband, Gary, had checked into the Holbrooke for a short stay and they were assigned Room 5. Enchanted by the hotel's gold rush era architecture, Mary began to take a number of photographs with her simple automatic camera using ordinary still photography film. A member of the hotel staff suggested that she might find the large iron doors in the basement to be of particular interest, these being the highly secure doors through which, it has been said, gold shipments from Grass Valley's gold mines once passed. Upon her attempting to photograph one of the iron doors, the lens of her camera began zooming in and out and she experienced the inescapable sensation that some invisible presence was standing directly behind her. Frightened, she immediately fled back upstairs.

Later that night, around one or two in the morning, Mary and Gary heard a strange noise in their bathroom followed by a frantic shaking back and forth of the door to their room as if someone was attempting to force the door open. At last, the shaking stopped only to commence again about two minutes later. Although there was a gap of about half of an inch between the bottom of the door and the floor through which they would have been able to see the feet or a shadow of anyone attempting to open the door in the well lit hallway, there was nothing to be seen. Gary courageously put his eye to the peephole while the door continued to shake. There was no one in the hallway.

None of this surprised me as previous guests staying in Room 5, careful to have securely locked the door before leaving the room, have reported being startled upon their return to find the door standing wide open. The television in Room 5 has been known to turn on by itself and, then, there was the time the curtains in the room flew out into the room, wrapping themselves around two guests who, at the time, had been sitting on the floor beneath the window.

When the Moores returned to their home in Southern California they had the photographs Mary had taken developed and printed. To their surprise, they discovered what appeared to be a ghost clearly visible in a photograph of the second floor staircase landing and the window above the landing. Appearing behind the right-hand center windowpane was the form of a man visible from only his waist upwards. It could not have been the reflection of anyone on the landing as Mary, who had taken the photograph, is not seen in the photograph. Furthermore, she had not seen the man in the window at the time she snapped the shutter.

After filming my portion of the *My Ghost Story* episode in Los Angeles, I was asked to help the show's film crew shoot B-roll footage at the Holbrooke at a later date. As a heavy snowstorm was expected the night of the B-roll shoot and the storm was predicted to continue into the next day, I was offered a room for two nights in the hotel. Hoping to experience something along the lines of what the Moores had recounted, I chose to spend those two nights in Room 5.

Although I had initially been told to expect the two-person film crew to arrive by noon, as their flight was canceled due to the inclement weather, I was told that they would, instead, travel to Grass Valley by car and that I should expect them to arrive at the hotel around midnight. I was the only guest in the hotel that night and I decided to wait up for the crew in my room. Twice, in the middle of the night, I

Mary Moore's photograph

Close-up from Mary Moore's photograph

194

clearly heard the sound of a conversation somewhere in the hotel hallways.

Each time that I heard the voices I felt certain it was the film crew and I got out of bed and made my way down the hall to the rooms which they were to occupy in order to ask what time in the morning they wanted to begin shooting. Each time I ventured out of my room, however, there was no one to be found anywhere in the entire second floor.

The film crew finally arrived the following afternoon and we quickly accomplished all of the required filming. As I had remained awake throughout the entire previous night, by 11:00 pm I was tired and I decided to go to bed while the film crew continued to film downstairs in the hope of capturing a ghost on film. I checked the clock as I finally got into bed. It was 11:30. No sooner had I noted the time than I heard the distinct sound of someone jumping up and down on old-fashioned bedsprings along with rhythmic shouting. This seemed odd as the mattress on my bed was quite new, as were, I later learned, all of the mattresses in the hotel. Although I found myself speculating as to the source of the sounds, I was far too tired to attempt an investigation and I promptly fell asleep.

The next morning, at breakfast, I met a party of four women who had spent the night in

Room 18, they being the only other guests booked in the hotel that night other than the film crew and myself. When they learned why I was there, one of the ladies said, "We need to tell you what happened last night."

It was 11:30 that night when they heard the same strange sounds which I had heard. They knew it was 11:30 as their television was on and *The Tonight Show* had just begun. Curious, they cautiously emerged from their room and followed the sound down the hallway until, by one of the ladies placing her ear to the door of the room at the end of the hallway, Room 15, they determined that the sounds of someone jumping up and down on a bed were coming from inside that room, an unoccupied room which had not been booked that night, a room with a particularly intriguing history.

Years before, a guest staying in Room 15 had enquired the next morning as to whether there had been an earthquake during the night. Upon learning that there been no earthquake, he responded, "I don't want to even think about any other explanation. In the middle of the night my bed began to jump up and down off the floor!"

If his experience that night was due to ghost children leaping about on his bed, apparently one or more of the ghost children has been known to venture out at times beyond the hotel building. A guest staying in the Pursell House, located at back of the Holbrooke property, told me of how, one night, her bed in the Purcell House began to shake up and down as if in an extreme earthquake. And members of the hotel staff have, more than once, observed the imprint of a small head to appear on the pillow of a freshly made bed in one of the Purcell House rooms.

Following the initial airing of the *My Ghost Story* episode concerning the Holbrooke, a tour guest asked me to show her the door to Room 5 which the Moores had twice observed to shake violently. As I stood with my back to the door, recounting the ghostly happenings said to have occurred inside Room 5, my guests appeared to be completely spellbound by my story. It was only after I had finished that a guest explained the reason for their extreme fascination. As I had been speaking, both she and her sister had clearly seen the doorknob to Room 5 turning back and forth. I quickly suggested that someone was, no doubt, in the room playing a joke on us. Upon checking at the front desk, however, we were told that no one had booked Room 5 that night and we were shown that both keys to the room were in the pigeonhole for Room 5 situated behind the desk.

It was also during that night's tour that we discovered the basement staircase to be blocked by two large armchairs and a furniture dolly; something which was to reoccur more than once in the months to come although, each time, all of the members of the hotel staff swore they had nothing to do with it.

Perhaps the ghosts of the Holbrooke still enjoy their earthly pleasures. A man in formal attire can sometimes be seen standing just outside Room 15 contentedly filling the hallway with the smell of cigar smoke; while, just around the corner and down the hall, the strains of phantom organ music have been heard emanating from within the walls of Room 12, a room which, appropriately enough, in years past, was named for the gold rush era singer, dancer and actress, Lotta Crabtree.

The distinct sound of a vacuum cleaner has been heard in an upstairs hallway in the small hours of the night although no housekeeping work is done at night and a vacuum cleaner was once observed making its way down a hotel hallway without anyone operating it.

The ghost children and the gentleman with the cigar are not, however, the only phantoms to prowl the hotel corridors.

There is the mysterious woman attired in a white Gibson Girl style blouse and a long wine colored shirt. When, years ago, a bartender observed her floating up the staircase to the second floor, he attempted to follow her as she proceeded down a hallway only to find, upon turning a corner, that she had vanished. When he reported the incident to the hotel manger, the manager casually replied, "Yes. That happens all the time."

And, then, there are specific rooms which seem to be particularly favored by the hotel's more restless spirits.

A guest staying in Room 16, who had a habit of sleeping with a pillow clutched between his arms and head, reported having had the pillow rudely ripped out from under his head by an unseen entity.

The drawers in an armoire in Room 2 have been known to open of their own accord.

A picture on a wall in Room 11, one day, rose up off the hook it on which it had been hanging and flung itself across the room.

A guest staying in Room 10 told me of the night she heard footsteps on the balcony outside her room. When she went out onto the balcony to investigate, not only was no one there but, upon returning back into the room, she discovered that the sheets, the blankets and the bedspread had all been pulled from her bed and deposited into three separate piles on the floor.

If you want to improve your chances of having a ghostly encounter at the Holbrooke, you might consider asking to stay in Room 9. From time to time, spirits have been seen passing through its locked door, the lights have been known to turn on by themselves in the locked and unoccupied room and guests have sometimes heard the lyrical voice of a woman singing; perhaps the voice of the ghostly maid, a most fastidious housekeeper, who has been known to sometimes pick up after sloppy guests.

A female guest, an army officer, after spending the night in Room 9, asked Eleanor the next morning, "Do people come into the rooms at night and do things?"

"I certainly hope not!" Eleanor replied. "Why do you ask?"

"I'm a bit of a slob" the lady explained. Her way of unpacking was to simply dump the entire contents of her luggage out onto the floor and that was what she had done. Upon awakening that morning, however, she found that all of her clothing and other personal items had either been hung up in the closet, been placed neatly in the dresser drawers or had been carefully arranged upon the top of the dresser.

The army officer's experience would not be at all unique. Guests often tell of seeing the ghostly maid, a short woman wearing a long dress with a bustle, her blonde hair pulled back into a bun, tidying up the room in the middle of the night or making the bed while the guest is still in it!

Though highly efficient and helpful to the guests of whom she approves, the ghostly maid can be roused to anger regarding those of whom she does not approve. On one occasion a guest who had carefully unpacked her luggage upon her arrival was dismayed upon awakening in the morning to find that all of her belongings had been roughly crammed back into her suitcase.

The ghostly maid has also been known to quickly retaliate if one is so gouch as to make a "dumb blond" joke — a most serious lapse in judgment as a member of the housekeeping staff, upon making such a joke, learned the hard way when she was immediately struck on the head with an old-fashioned hairpin. Moments later, she caught a brief glimpse of a blonde woman in Victorian attire flit around a corner.

The phantom maid seems, however, to have a sense of humor. While making the bed in Room 9 one day, a housekeeper was surprised to find the key to Room 8, situated across the hall, hidden within the bedding. On that same day, the key to Room 9 was found hidden within the bedding in Room 8.

When Ian Garfinkel, a previous owner of the hotel, first took charge of the Holbrooke he decided to spend a night in each of the rooms in order to better assess what changes and improvements needed to be made in the various rooms. On the night in which he stayed in Room 9 he moved a chair, upon which he had placed a stack of legal papers related to the sale of the hotel, to one side of the bed. Upon awakening the next morning, he was surprised to see that the chair had been moved to the foot of the bed. "It was as if the ghost had been sitting there all night watching me," he later recalled.

Even more disturbing was the fact that a heavy mirror which had been hanging over a basin the previous night was now lying in the sink. The nail upon which it had hung was still securely embedded in an upright position in the wall and the wire on the back of the mirror's frame was intact. "The only way that mirror could have come off the wall," Ian stated, "was if someone had lifted it off of the nail and placed it in the sink."

Most of the hotel's ghosts are usually quite passive and benign in their behavior. However, a few of the Holbrooke's spirits have been known to take a more active and personal interest in the living; spirits which can, at times, be quite frightening; for behind those locked doors, when guests feel safe and cozy, it is not unknown for spirits to pay them a visit.

Consider the ordeal experienced by the guest staying in Room 16 who, upon returning to her bed after a late night trip to the bathroom, without warning, felt something pressing down on top of her. For over an hour and a half she was unable either to move or to scream until, mercifully, the unseen wraith vanished as unexpectedly as it had appeared.

Almost as frightening was the time a former owner of the Holbrooke spent the night in Room 14. No sooner had he gotten into bed than he saw the sheets and covers on one side of him lift up into the air followed by the mattress on that side of the bed depressing as if someone had crawled into bed with him. The sheets and covers then floated back down onto the bed covering whoever or whatever it was that had decided to spend the night with him. The man never spent another night in his own hotel.

But it is down in the basement that hotel guests experience the greatest sense of dread, an eerie, unshakeable feeling that they are being watched. Footprints have appeared on the freshly vacuumed basement carpeting although no one had entered the basement following its morning cleaning. And it is there in the basement that a menacing looking cowboy stands sentinel, perhaps a guard from the days when gold shipments were said to have been transported through mining tunnels which opened into the Holbrooke's basement. Although so clearly observed as to be mistaken for a living person, the cowboy disappears from his knees downward. This same phantom was also independently seen on two separate occasions, by two different members of the hotel staff, leaning against a table in the North Star Hall, each witness describing him in exactly the same way. In these instances, however, the cowboy's entire body, including the lower portion of his legs, was clearly visible.

But it is the ladies' room which has the most ominous reputation. It is there that guests sometimes experience a sudden blast of cold air and it is there that the lights have been known to go out without warning. On other occasions women have complained of hearing a pounding on the iron doors which once opened onto a mining tunnel while male voices on the other side of those doors were heard to shout, "Let us in! Let us in!"

One day, an employee, upon entering the ladies' room, found that all three faucets were turned on in the unoccupied restroom. She turned off each tap and went into one of the stalls. A few moments later, all three faucets were back on again, the water surging full blast into the sinks.

The images of men dressed in clothing of the 1800's and another image, that of a woman of the Victorian era dressed in red, have, at times, been seen reflected in the ladies' room mirror.

A former desk clerk fearfully told me of the day she heard the distinct "click click" of a woman's high heels on the floor of the, otherwise, unoccupied ladies' room, quickly followed by the restroom door opening and closing by itself.

Most frightening of all was the day when a woman, upon entering a stall, found herself under attack as the stall began to violently shake. At the same time, a frantic pounding reverberated upon the stall walls. Fearing that a lunatic had entered the room, she threw open the stall door and ran out. No one was in the room and, as the restroom door opens outward, she would have seen it to be in the process of closing if anyone had, only moments before, fled the room.

Despite the recent remodeling of the hotel, the ghostly phenomena have continued unabated. A painter working on the second floor during the renovation process reported hearing the sound of someone whistling at a time when he was the only person in the entire hotel. And, despite each of the guestrooms being fitted with ultra secure magnetic strip key card locks, housekeepers have reported doors to rooms they were cleaning flying open without any discernible cause.

Determining the specific identity of any of the Holbrooke's resident ghosts or discovering why they may have chosen to remain is almost impossible but, in one case, we might be able to take an educated guess. Years ago a guest, upon being shown to her room, became terrified and refused to cross the threshold. Although invisible to anyone but her, she claimed that a wall in the room was sprayed with blood. While which room this was is unknown, it does suggest an event which took place at the Holbrooke on Sunday, April 17, 1927.

John Henry Martin, a forty-six-year-old Cornish miner, known locally as Jack, was, at the time, residing at the Holbrooke. He had checked in four days before upon returning from a trip he had taken to England to visit his mother and daughter. He had for many years lived at various times in Grass Valley and, for the last several years, he had worked as a professional gambler.

When that afternoon the hotel housekeeper found that the door to his room was bolted shut from the inside, preventing her from entering to clean the room, and no one answered her entreaties to let her in, she notified George Perkins, the hotel proprietor, who investigated. Peering through the transom over the door, Perkins encountered a grisly sight, Jack Martin lying on the floor in a pool of blood, his throat slashed, a straight razor by his side.

Dr. C. P. Jones was called and he gained entry into the locked room by way of a window.

While it was clear that Martin had taken his own life, those who entered his room and observed the scene were left momentarily puzzled. What was termed "a considerable sum of cash" was found on his person and he was known to have several thousand dollars on deposit at a local bank.

Gradually, the sad facts leading to his death became apparent. Several acquaintances had noticed that he had been acting strangely upon returning to Grass Valley. While traveling on the steamer home he had apparently suffered from hallucinations and he had become convinced that he was being followed and continually watched.

A suicide note scrawled in disjointed phrases explained it all.

"The watch on the suitcase is Bob Cruz's, Boston Ravine. I loaned 15 on it. Return it to him, Eddie.

"I don't know what's wrong. Somebody done me wrong. The money I got I made playing poker and the money I got in me I took to England and brought back again. I never done any wrong. The man put me to sign a paper when I went to get my passport lengthened out and I never read it and they done me in. I am going to end it all. They have wronged me. I should never been here. If I thought trouble nobody told me but can see it through. That fellow watching me on the boat and I been watched all the time. I don't know what the trouble is. Nobody told me anything. I never stole no money. I won all, or that I worked for, playing poker, running honest poker home games."

J Martin

And scrawled below his signature were two final lines.

"Good bye. Sorry anything like this happened. Good bye. All you will think better of me after finding the truth."

If, indeed, Jack Martin is one of the ghosts haunting the Holbrooke, let us hope, that by our having now heard his story, he may, at last, feel himself free to leave and find peace on "the other side."

Epilogue

The foregoing are but a few of the many ghosts to be encountered in Nevada City and Grass Valley. If you know of a haunting I have missed or if you have encountered one of the ghosts whose stories have been recounted herein, I would very much appreciate the opportunity to hear from you.

Please write to me at: mlyon@hauntedisles.com.

Mark Lyon

Called "a master storyteller" by the *Times Colonist* of Victoria, Canada; actor and playwright, Mark Lyon, has, for over twenty years, toured across North America and Ireland performing original one-man plays as well as having recounted true ghost stories on scores of television and radio programs. In 2012 Lyon was invited to perform his solo play, *Ghosties and Ghoulies and Long-Legged Beasties and Things that Go Bump in the Night* at Ireland's prestigious Listowel Writers Week Festival.

Lyon wrote and narrated the film docudrama, *Phantoms of the Holbrooke*, and he is the author of *The Young Ghost Hunter's Handbook*. In his monthly podcast, *The Other Realm*, Lyon recounts true tales of ghosts and other supernatural encounters curated from across the globe.